The Peoples of the Great North

Art and Civilisation of Siberia

Publishing Director : Jean-Paul Manzo
Text : Valentina Gorbatcheva, Marina Federova
Translation from French : Mike Darton
Design and layout : Cédric Pontes
Publishing assistant : Séverine Corson

Photograph credits :
Magalie Delorme : 8, 9, 21, 36, 151, 165, 186, 193, 196, 226, 227
Marine Le Berre Semenov : 2, 6, 7, 10, 11,16, 17, 18, 20, 53, 56, 134, 136, 137, 150, 152, 156, 157, 175, 176, 179, 182, 183, 197, 216, 217, 218, 219.

We are very grateful to the ethnological Museum of St Petersburg

Parkstone Press LTD
Printed and bound in Singapore
ISBN 1 85995 479 0

Valentina Gorbatcheva   Marina Federova

The Peoples of the Great North
Art and Civilisation of Siberia

Avec le concours scientifique de
Marine Le Berre Semenov

PARKSTONE PRESS

1 Herd of reindeer crossing a river.
Chukchi.
2 The tundra under the spring snows
(May).

Introduction

The Evenki, the Yukhagirs, the Chukchis, the Koryaks, the Nenets, the Nanai people, the Yakuts, the Tuva people . . . Cradle of many cultures, Siberia constitutes an area that is rich in human traditions as diverse and changeable over time as the region itself. The native inhabitants of Siberia, dwellers in the lands of far-northern and far-eastern Russia – by tradition reindeer-herders, horse-breeders, hunters of marine mammals and fishermen-hunters – have, over the millennia, evolved the means by which human communities may survive in this vast desert of extreme climatic conditions in northern Asia. Colonization by incoming cultures has in many cases caused a significant decline in the fortunes of such groups. Those with the fewest numbers today may yet witness for themselves the extinction of their ancestral cultures.

Following a concise overview of the relationship between the climate, the terrain and the peoples, and a summary of the historical background from which those peoples stemmed, this book's constant endeavour is to enable the reader to enter fully into the traditional world and shamanist mindset of the original inhabitants of 'Russian' Asia.

NATURE, AND THE SETTLEMENT OF SIBERIA

SIBERIA: THE GEOGRAPHICAL FACTS

Understood for close on three centuries now to be no more than a geographical extension of the Russian state, Siberia stretches from the icy Arctic Ocean in the north to borders with Kazakhstan, with Mongolia and with China in the south, from the great chain of the Ural Mountains in the west all the way over to the Pacific Ocean in the east. Within that span it covers no fewer than eight different time zones and around 20° latitude (between 50° and 70° North) – and thus actually represents more than two-thirds of the entire territory of Russia: some 4.9 million miles^2 (12.7 million km^2).

Many Europeans think of Siberia as one huge wilderness remote and hostile to human habitation, mostly iced over, darkened by the polar night for a good proportion of the year. And yet Siberia is nothing if not diverse. From north to south there are a number of large areas that are completely different from each other in climate and terrain and thus in the local flora and fauna. The Arctic wastes shade into the tundra with its permafrost; further south, the tundra in turn shades into the slightly warmer zones where scrubby trees will grow; further south still is the evergreen coniferous forest of the taiga; continuing south, there are the fertile steppes and then the arid steppes – and all these various ecological areas come with their own topographical relief, from low-level flatlands to massively towering peaks.

Occupying the greater part of this vast landmass, the central Siberian plateau is bounded to the north, east and south by an enormous amphitheatre of mountain chains. To the north and east are the mountains of Verkhoyansk, which at their highest reach 9,097feet (2,389metres). Forming Siberia's southern boundary are the Sayan mountains (9,612feet/2,930metres) and the ranges of the Altai (which at Mt Belukha top out at 14,783feet/4,506metres). Within these various chains lie the sources of the three great Siberian rivers, the Ob, the Yenisey (a name derived from Evenki ioanessi 'great river'), and the Lena. These rivers are frozen over for much of the year – between October/November and May/June – but at other times flow powerfully across Siberia for about 2,500miles (4,000kilometres) until they reach the cold Arctic Ocean.

3 Eskimo (Uit) woman in traditional costume.

9

The Arctic Ocean to the north of Siberia is itself divided into several regional seas –from west to east, the Kara Sea, the Laptev Sea and the East Siberian Sea – which are likewise choked with a thick blanket of ice for at least ten months of the year. The summer period of remission is brief: just the remaining two months, July and August.

In these northerly latitudes, the ground surface – permanently frozen – is mostly shingle, perhaps covered in algae, lichens and mosses. This is the true Arctic wilderness and characterizes most of the islands, especially those off the coast of the Taimyr Peninsula. Seals, walruses, belugas and polar bears populate the coastline.

As distance increases from the north pole southwards, the Arctic wilderness turns into the tundra – a bare region in which only lichens, mosses and short, scrubby trees (dwarf species of birch or willow, mainly) shroud the ground, with some spiky plants and Arctic grasses. Winter in the tundra is lengthy – between eight and ten months – and cold. At the end of November the sun dips below the horizon and does not return. This is the polar night, which in the tundra lasts for two or three months (compared with up to six months in the Arctic wilderness). Then finally, in January, the sun reappears once more, and the days little by little lengthen even as the nights little by little become shorter. This goes on until, from sometime in May to sometime in July, the sun doesn't leave the sky at all.

Summer in the Arctic is not so much warm as brisk – temperatures average from 5- 12°C (40-68°F) – and short. Towards mid-August, heralding the end of summertime, the tundra takes on its autumnal coloration. Leaves on the woody plants turn golden, the lichens and mosses turn grey, while the wild mushrooms sprout in abundance and the berries ripen in a vast moving red and orange carpet.

4 Carved walrus tusk, in colour. Fragment, 1930s, Chukchi, Chukotskiy Peninsula. Walrus tusk ivory, 57 x 6 cm.

The tundra is the home of the reindeer (caribou), of the Arctic wolf, the wolverine (glutton), the Arctic fox, the lemming, the great white owl, and the ptarmigan (the gallinaceous bird that, unlike any other, winters by hiding itself under the snow). In spring, the tundra welcomes the arrival of the many migratory birds – geese, swans, ducks, terns, gulls and others – that come to breed.

The terrain tends to be marshy, with a scattering of thousands of little lakes of no real depth. Baron Eddel, a traveller who a hundred years or so ago explored the lower reaches of the Indigirka and the Kolyma Rivers, recalled in his memoirs that 'to draw a map of all these lakes, all you need to do is dip a paintbrush in blue watercolour and bespeckle the paper all over with it'. The tundra is swampy because of the presence beneath the topsoil of permafrost – a stratum of soil frozen solid over thousands of years sometimes to a depth of 1,000feet (300metres) or more, whereas the topsoil itself may be no more than a foot (30centimetres) deep. The permafrost is impervious, which means that although annual rainfall may be comparatively low, the water cannot drain away or be absorbed. Nor does it evaporate, because the air is already extremely humid and the heat is not sufficient.

5 Bear with a fish in its mouth. Figurine, 1903, Koryak. Walrus tusk ivory, 8 x 5 cm.

6 The Lena under ice and snow.

7 The Lena on the break-up of the ice.

The southern boundary of the permafrost – a line that actually runs through a little less than two-thirds of the area covered by the Russian state – lies north of the valleys of the lower Tunguska (a tributary of the Yenisey) and the Vilyuy (a tributary of the Lena).

It is in the north-east of Siberia that the permafrost is most extensive. To the north of Yakutia the subsoil keeps turning up the fossilized remains of animals – whole cemeteries of mammoths trapped in thick layers of frozen sediments, their bones and their ivory tusks forming colossal repositories.

It is also in Yakutia that the coldest place in the Northern hemisphere is located – at Oymyakon, in the Verkhoyansk mountains. Here, the average temperature in January is somewhere between –48°C and –50°C (–54°F and –58°F), occasionally getting down to as low as –70°C (–94°F). However, the air is so dry, and there is no wind at all, so these temperatures do not feel as extreme as they might.

Further south, a change in vegetation indicates a difference in the pre-vailing climate and conditions. The number of dwarf trees and bushes increases greatly. This is an intermediate zone between tundra and taiga (which many people think of as an individual zone in its own right). Continuing south, the vegetation diversifies. The trees become more numerous and grow much taller. Finally, the environment is that of the taiga – the huge northern forest that cloaks the greater part of Russia.

Comprising mostly conifers (larch, pine and Siberian cedar) but also in the north birch, willow and aspen, in the south and west deciduous species, the taiga forests are home to an important group of larger predatory animals (bears, wolverines, wolves and lynxes), foraging omnivores (foxes, sables, polecats, weasels, ermines, mink and martens), ungulates (deer and elk) and birds (capercaillies, partridges, woodpeckers and nutcrackers). Winters in this region are very long and very cold. Summers, however, can be warm in the central part of the region where the annual range of temperatures can be as wide as 100 degrees on the Celsius scale (180 degrees on the Fahrenheit scale) – propitious times for the insects, especially for the mosquitoes, midges and flies for which the tundra, with its multitudinous marshes and lakes, has been the ideal breeding-ground.

8 Lake Lama, on the Taimyr Peninsula.

9 Looking for water in the Lena. Khamarhatta village, Yakutia.

10 Marshy areas in the tundra.

11 The Lena.

12 Yukaghir man's costume. Yakutia, Kolyma Oblast. Incorporating the skins and furs of reindeer, seal, dog, wolverine and squirrel; linen and cotton cloth; reindeer hair; and glass beads. Coat length: 100 cm; circumference at the chest: 86 cm; at the trouser-legs: 22 cm.

13 Hunter with the skin of a fox he has killed. 1979, Chukchi, Magadan, village of Vankarem.

14 Box for containing vessels. Evenki,
Sakhalin island, 1962. Wood, cured
hide (leather), reindeer fur, sable fur,
bearskin, cloth, matt canvas,
17 x 33 cm.

15 Yakut trinket-box. Yakutsk, 1845.
Mammoth ivory, 16 x 10.5 x 6.5 cm.

16 The taiga (central Yakutia).

17 The taiga, in the area of Kolyma
(Yukaghirs).

18 Swampy area in the region of
Yakutsk.

19 Pipe. 1906, Koryak, the Anadyr
area. Walrus ivory, length: 14.2 cm.

Further south still, the taiga gives way first to the fertile steppes and then to the arid steppes – areas typical of northern Central Asia and Mongolia. Here, the climate is by no means unpleasant: summers are fairly long and warm, and the rainfall is light although the prevailing winds tend to be strong. Much of the steppes is covered by vast prairies of tall grasses growing on humus-rich fertile soil.

It is an area well suited to farming, both of crops and of livestock. But there is plenty of wildlife too: marmots, voles and fieldmice, hamsters, jerboas, hares, foxes, saiga antelopes and badgers. Birds of the steppes include bustards, kestrels, Asiatic white cranes and many more.

20 Marshy areas in the tundra.

21 Lake Baikal.

22 Chukchi woman with children at the entrance to the *yarang.* Yakutia, 1925–1926.

23 Koryak water-scoop. Kamchatka, 1909–1911. Ram's-horn, 14.5 x 12 cm; diameter of scoop: 10.4 cm.

24 Koryak spoon. Kamchatka, 1909–1911. Ram's-horn, length: 15.9 cm.

25 'Flying object' and pen. Eskimo (Uit), Chukchi Peninsula, 3rd–4th century AD. Walrus ivory, length: i) 6.2 cm, ii) 13.7 cm.

Amid the arid steppes north of Mongolia, over a length of an extraordinary 400miles (635kilometres), stretches the largest inland source of fresh water in the world: Lake Baikal. In places it is 5,300feet (1,620metres) deep. A miracle of nature, Lake Baikal provides essential water for all kinds of local populations – including of course the creatures that live in it, which are now regrettably under severe threat from the pollution exuded into the lake as effluent from the timber workings up the rivers that flow into it.

The most easterly part of Russia is an area drained largely by rivers that flow out into the Pacific Ocean – rivers such as the Anadyr in the north and the Amur in the south. In the area around the Amur (which for a time forms the boundary with China), the climate and the overall humidity are favourable to the growth of mixed forest, particularly of broadleaved trees like limes, aspens or oaks. The wildlife here is much the same as in the taiga, with the addition of the Asiatic tiger, the leopard, the civet, the genet, the goral (a goat-like antelope related to the chamois), the sika deer and a great number of bird species.

Siberia is rich in natural resources. It has minerals that can be extracted – gold, silver, tin, diamonds, nickel and phosphates; it has abundant means for supplying energy – huge reserves of oil and petroleum and of natural gas, extensive coal seams, and a great number of fast-flowing waterways; and it has a wealth of other useful and commercial materials – the timber in its forests and the pelts of its animals. In many ways, then, it is Russia's warehouse of goodies, contributing around one-fifth of the state's overall gross national product.

And yet this is the territory used by the Tsars as a penal colony, a vast concentration camp for 'internal exiles'. This too is where, simply because it contained all those goodies, massive migrations of people were organized and resettled during the whole of the period of Soviet domination, despite the generally inhospitable nature of much of the territory to human occupation. Close on 32 million souls were sent to take part in exploiting Siberia's resources, and many of them (and their descendants) are still there, in the thousands of towns, industrial centres and mining camps set up specifically – places like Vorkuta, Noril'sk, Novosibirsk, Krasnoyarsk, Bratsk, Irkutsk, Kemerovo, Prokop'yevsk, Angarsk, Komsomolsk-on-Amur, Yakutsk, Petropavlovsk-Kamchatskiy, Magadan, Khabarovsk, Vladivostok and Ussuriysk.

THE FIRST HUMAN COLONIZERS

Penal colony, place of banishment, 'northern Eldorado' for millions of Soviet migrants – Siberia today is populated by members of considerably more than a hundred different ethnic groups from all over what used to be the Soviet Union. It is not altogether surprising, then, that this vast northerly and easterly area is far less well known for being the cradle of cultures some of which are many thousands of years old. Representatives of around thirty of these aboriginal groups still live in the region, although some of the groups now comprise very few individuals (and are accordingly lumped together by some anthropologists under misleadingly blanket-style descriptive names, like 'the northerly folk').

The fact is that from the far north down to the southern steppes and across to the most easterly region, Siberia displays a rich panorama of local cultures, traditions, languages and different ways of life. The history of these aboriginal groups, however, has in general been as misunderstood, or as unconscionably misinterpreted, as has in times not so long past the history of such other aboriginal peoples as the Native American Indians or the Australian Aborigines. Now, at the dawning of the 21st century, this heritage of human endeavour through the millennia is fast eroding away and may soon be lost for ever.

The earliest incomers

Archaeologists have turned up evidence of the presence of human residents in this part of the world as early as in the Upper Palaeolithic age between 20,000 and 25,000 years ago. Scattered remains throughout Siberia and along the northerly coastline indicate that by Neolithic times much of northern Asia was inhabited by people with some pretensions to culture, for they certainly seem, all those thousands of years ago, to have differentiated between the material and the spiritual sides of life, and to have appreciated their own forms of art.

26 Evenki summer camp. Beginning of the 20th century.

27 Yakut toys: i) reindeer, ii) seal. i) Yakutia, ii) Turukhansk region; i) 1908, ii) 1903. Wood, length: i) 22 cm, ii) 18 cm; height: i) 4 cm, ii) 13 cm.

28 Protection for the hands when using a bow and arrow. Chukchi, Uit, Chukchi Peninsula, i) 2nd to 4th century AD, ii) 1904–1907. Walrus ivory, skin, length: i) 11.3 cm, ii) 13 cm.

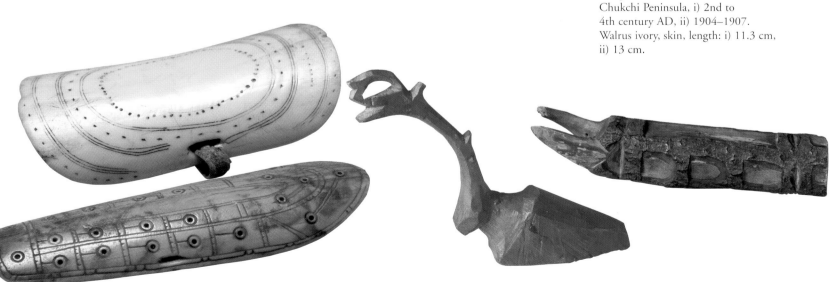

The steppes of southern Siberia and the area around Lake Baikal were first settled by tribes who were livestock-herders and crop-growers. In the neighbouring regions of the taiga, people lived instead by hunting and fishing. It is probable that the communities in what is now Yakutia and the residents of the Baikal area maintained fairly close connections, which would account for the well-established cultural group that occupied the area between the Angara and Lena rivers. Archaeological evidence relating to this group is fairly plentiful, and includes rock carvings that appear to reveal particular aspects of their spiritual beliefs (involving rites of passage, Neolithic hunting rituals, and so forth).

The regions of the tundra to the north-east of Siberia were occupied by nomadic tribes who lived by hunting reindeer (rather than herding them) and by fishing. Sites discovered between the rivers Olenëk and Kolyma have proved that the ancestors of today's Yukaghirs lived by hunting and fishing, in total isolation, from the Neolithic period for at least another thousand years.

Elsewhere in the north-east were regions occupied by ancestors of the present-day Chukchis and Eskimos, who were able to live a settled, residential life because they depended on the resources of the sea. In time, the way of life of these marine predators became widespread, from the shores of the Bering Sea over the length of the Arctic coastline.

Inland, many communities at first lived a nomadic form of existence based upon hunting wild reindeer. The 'domestication' of the reindeer – or at least the discovery of the way of life that involved herding the semi-domesticated creature – was a highly progressive stage in the overall history of humans' successfully taking up residence in the tundra and the taiga.

The great age of human migration in Central Asia fell between the 10th and 13th centuries AD. This was the time when an influx of new people into Siberia from the south pushed the original inhabitants there northwards and eastwards. Palaeo-Asiatic groups such as the Chukchis and Koryaks, and Tungusic tribespeople such as the Evenki and the Eveni, formerly resident in what today is Yakutia, thus found themselves hounded from their homelands and forced towards the northern and eastern margins by the ancestors of modern Yakuts – who had themselves been pushed northwards by Mongol-speaking invaders.

29 Schematic representations of the human form. Eskimo (Uit), Chukchi Peninsula, 3rd–4th century AD. Walrus ivory, height: i) 4.7 cm, ii) 3.7 cm, iii) 3.8 cm.

30 Eskimo (Uit) children.

Until the 16th and 17th centuries, the peoples of Siberia had no contact at all with any European civilization. All were isolated, each community generally maintaining some form of relations only with neighbouring communities, and then often only if those communities were from the same cultural background. The names these people of the north give themselves in their own languages frequently bear witness to this aspect of primal isolation: most of the tribal names mean simply 'the people'. In this way, the Chukchis call themselves the *Lyg'oravetlat*, and the Eskimos think of themselves as the *Uit*, *Yuit* or *Yupik*, all of which mean 'the (real) people'.

Likewise, the Nenets know themselves as *Khasava* 'people', whereas the Olchi people, the Oroki and the Orochon people reckon that they are all *Nani* which, like *Nanai* – for several decades now the official name of their neighbouring tribal group, otherwise known as the Gold people – would seem to mean 'the people of the soil' (just as in English *human* may be related to *humus*).

When the Russians took over Siberia and its inhabitants, they tended to rechristen the groups they came across, often borrowing the neighbouring people's name for each community rather than the indigenous name. This is, for example, how the peoples now known as Yakuts and Yukaghirs got their current names. As far as they are concerned, they are the *Sakha* and the *Odul* respectively – but in Evenki they were the *Yakut* 'the yak (or cow) people' and the *Yukaghirs* 'the ice dwellers' – and that is the way they are now known all over the world. Similarly, the peoples known by much of the world (but not in countries where there are Lapps) as Khanty and Mansis recognize themselves only as *Ostyaks* or *Vogul* people. The Eveni think of themselves as the *Lamut*.

31 Sculpture in miniature: representations of aquatic birds, with a clasp in the form of a bear. Eskimo (Uit), Chukchi Peninsula, 3rd–4th century AD. Walrus ivory. Diameter of the bird figurines: I) 3.2 cm, ii) 2.8 cm; height: I) 3.2 cm, ii) 3.5 cm; length of the clasp: 5.7 cm.

32 Yakut carrying straw for sale.

Diverse environments and ways of life

From west to east inside the zone of the tundra that borders the coast of the Arctic Ocean, nomadic groups who live by herding reindeer, by hunting and by fishing, successively neighbour and occasionally overlap with each other. In that part which is in Russian Europe, on the Kola Peninsula, live the **Saami** (or Sami), better known as the Lapps, who also live in the north of Finland, Norway and Sweden. From the banks of the Dvina to the Yenisey, and particularly on the Yamal Peninsula, live the **Nenets**, whose territory thus just reaches into the Taimyr Peninsula – the area which, since prehistoric times, has been the home of the **Nganassani**, the most northerly-based people in the whole of Russian Asia. The area from the River Taz to the River Turukhan (a tributary of the Yenisey) is the home of the **Selkup**. Now almost disappeared, the **Enets** – culturally closely related to both the Nenets and the Nganassani – live along the banks of the Yenisey, where they come into contact with the **Dolgans**, a relatively new ethnic group which have not been around for much more than a couple of centuries, and which derive from combined Yakut, Evenki and Russian antecedents. The Dolgans are also prevalent in the north-east of Yakutia. Displaced ever northwards by the Yakuts infiltrating from the south, groups of **Evenki** established themselves on the lower courses of the Lena, which forms the western boundary of an enormous territory dominated for at least one millennium, as far as the River Kolyma, by the **Yukaghirs**. Of the Yukaghirs there are now only a few hundred left, generally in the Kolyma Basin not far from the mouth of the Alazeya, although some live further south in the taiga on the banks of the River Yasachnaya (Upper Kolyma). The **Eveni** people, also displaced by incoming Yakuts, once lived in what are now the lands of the Yukaghirs in northern Yakutia, and as late as the 19th century found themselves pushed all the way to the extreme north-east to live among the **Chukchis** and their neighbours to the south, in Kamchatka, the reindeer-herding **Koryaks**.

Some of these ethnic groups of the tundra are also represented in the more southerly zones of the taiga, including, for instance, the Nenets, the Eveni and the Evenki. The Evenki, in fact, are scattered across a vast area bounded in the west by a line between the Rivers Ob and Irtysh, in the east by the coastline of the Sea of Okhotsk, and in the south by the Upper Tunguska (a tributary of the Yenisey), the Angara, Lake Baikal, and by the Amur River.

33 Eveni, Okhotsk region, 1896–1897.

34 Eveni women with their children.

35 Evenki group of women and
children, Yenisey Province.

The taiga affords a fairly good living for the nomadic peoples who hunt and fish, or who hunt when they are not herding reindeer. In the west, on the plain of the Ob, is the land of the **Khanty** and the **Mansis** – closely related culturally and linguistically – who have a variety of lifestyles, based on hunting, fishing, herding reindeer and breeding other live-stock. The non-nomadic (residential) **Kets** hunt and fish on the edges of the Yenisey. Pouring up from the south during the 14th century, the **Yakuts** established themselves firmly on the middle courses of the Lena. This horse- and cattle-breeding people finally occupied an area as large as the Indian subcontinent, bordered to the north by the Arctic Ocean, pushing before them to the north and east those groups that had been there first – the Evenki, the Eveni, the Yukaghirs and the Chukchis.

36 Lake Baikal: the traders of Omul.

37 Chukchis in traditional costume.

38 Quiver and arrows. Chukchi, the Anadyr area, 1904–1907. Dried sealskin, stitched with reindeer-hide; wood, metal, bone, feathers. Quiver length: 88 cm, width: 21.5 cm; length of arrows: 76.5 cm, 79 cm, 77.3 cm, 76.5 cm.

In the south of Siberia, towards the frontier with Mongolia between the Ob and the Yenisey, the **Altai people** (or **Oirot**), the **Tuva people** (or **Tuvinians** or **Soyot**), a little further northwards the **Khakass people** and, to the east of Lake Baikal, the **Buryats** are all specialists in raising horned animals Mongolian-style. Yet the **Karagas people** (or **Tofalars**) – a very small ethnic group to the west of Lake Baikal – herd reindeer and live by hunting and fishing in the taiga.

The peoples of the Pacific coastline, from the Bering Strait in the north down to the Chinese border, mostly hold to a traditionally non-nomadic (residential) lifestyle that involves hunting marine mammals. These include the **Aleuts** of the Commander (Komandorski) Islands, separated from their ethnic brethren on the other islands to the east, the Aleutian Islands, not only by the Russian-American border but also by the international date-line. In this way they are very like the **Uit** (**Yuit** or Eskimos) who live on the shores of the Bering Strait, cut off from their ethnic cousins in Alaska and Canada. Inhabitants here additionally include communities of **Chukchis** and **Koryaks**, smaller groups of semi-nomadic Eveni people living on the shores of the Sea of Okhotsk (in the Magadan region), and, on the island of Sakhalin, the **Nivkhi** (or **Gilyaks**).

Finally, still in the extreme east of Siberia, but further south around the border with China, is where the **Eveni** and the **Evenki** live, in close touch with the **Olchi**, the **Orochon** people, the **Oroki**, the **Negidal people** and the **Udekhe**, all originally inhabitants of the Amur Basin. Before the Russians took over, these semi-nomadic groups who depend on hunting and fishing were for centuries, if not millennia, under the thumb of their equally dominant neighbours, the Chinese.

39 The people of the tundra.
Chukchis, the Anadyr area, 1986.

Linguistic links

Although the peoples of Siberia may no longer live in what used to be their ancestral territories and are scattered in groups here and there in no particular pattern, they may nonetheless be regarded as stemming ultimately from

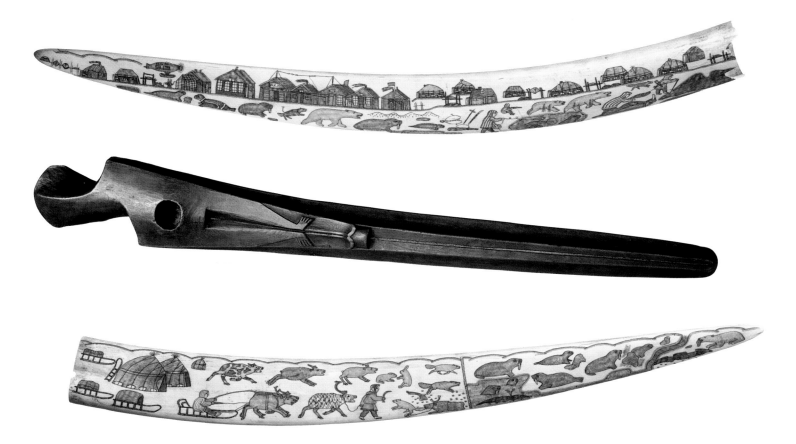

40 Carved walrus tusk in colour (primary face). Chukchi, Chukchi Peninsula, 1930s. Walrus ivory, length: 62 cm, width: 6 cm.

41 Arrow. Aleuts, the Commander Islands. Wood and bone.

42 Carved walrus tusk in colour (secondary face). Fragment, Chukchi, Chukchi Peninsula, 1930s. Length: 62 cm, width: 6 cm.

only eight independent 'nations', based not on racial characteristics but on language families. Most, in fact, belong to one or other of just two – the Uralic and the Altaic language super-families.

In the west of Siberia, the Uralic super-family is represented by the Khanty and the Mansis who are related to the Finno-Ugric branch (which includes Lapps and Finns), and by their northern neighbours the Nenets, the Enets, the Nganassani and the Selkup who make up the Samoyedic branch. The Evenki, the Eveni and the peoples of the Amur region all belong to the Tungusic family, a branch of the Altaic super-family, which also includes in its Turkic branch the Yakuts, the Khakass people, the Tuva people, the Altai people, the Dolgans, the Shorians and the Karagas people, and in its Mongolian branch the Buryats. The Kets around the Yenisey and the Nivkhi on Sakhalin each speak a language that appears not to be related to any other. Independent of the Uralic and Altaic super-family communities listed above, the peoples of north-eastern Siberia form three different linguistic groups: Chukchi-Koryak-Kamchadal (occasionally referred to as 'palaeo-Asiatic') which includes the tongues of the Chukchis, the Koryaks, the Kereks and the Itelmen (the latter of whom speak Kamchadal); the Eskimo-Aleut group which combines the Uit and the Aleuts; and finally the Yukaghir-Chuvantsi group which self-evidently comprises the languages of the Yukaghirs and the Chuvantsi, although these two may be said to be grouped together only by convention.

The majority of the ethnic groups in Siberia have a couple of major factors in common: an area of dispersal so wide as to be significant for the continuing survival of each group, and the varying influences of unrelated neighbouring groups on the larger groups that do live as ethnic communities. So, for example, the Koryaks – like the Chukchis or the Eveni people – may themselves be divided into two groups:

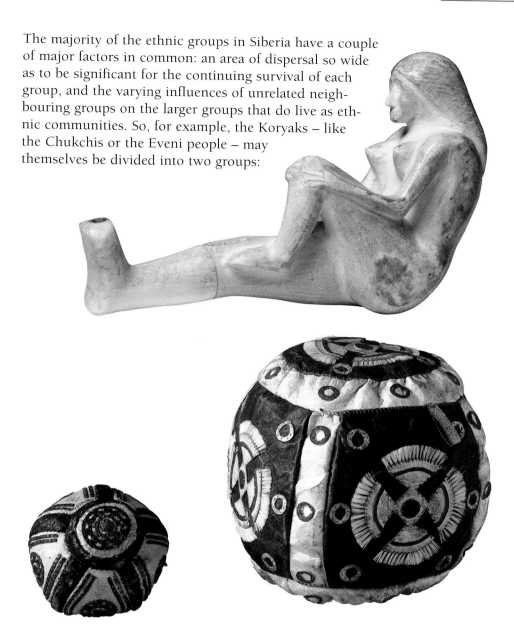

one that lives on the coast by hunting marine mammals and by fishing, the other that lives as nomads who herd reindeer and follow them inland in due season. Such groups, although originally speaking precisely the same language tend after all this time to speak different dialects of the parent language. And in the case of the Yukaghirs, the dialects have become so different and so mutually unintelligible that some linguistic anthropologists prefer to regard the Yukaghirs of the taiga who live by hunting and fishing as a completely different ethnic group from the Yukaghirs of the tundra who live by herding reindeer.

But no matter how different the languages and the corresponding dialects have become, no matter what other linguistic barriers there are between the residents of Siberia, it remains a salient fact that today it is (and has for a time been) the Russian language that has in many areas displaced the ancestral languages for ordinary daily purposes. The result of compulsory assimilation programmes and the deliberate blurring of ethnic differences, it may well be that even now the numbers of speakers of some of these tongues are so few as not to be able to prevent them from dying out altogether.

43 Pipe in the form of a female outline. Koryak. Walrus ivory.

44 Balls for playing games, i) with the feet, ii) with the hands. Chukchi, Eskimo (Uit), Chukchi Peninsula, i) 1974, ii) 1904–1907. Sealskin and seal hair, stitched with reindeer-hide. Diameter: i) 58 cm, ii) 25 cm.

45 Child learning how to throw the
lasso. Chukchi.

Cultures on the edge of extinction

With a total of some 32 million inhabitants, Siberia can nonetheless boast no more than a million and a half of the aboriginal populations. Indeed, apart from the Buryats, the Yakuts, the Tuva people, the Khakass people, the Shorians and the Altai people, no fewer than 26 other ethnic groups are officially (according to figures taken from the Soviet census in 1989) recorded as 'ultra-minorities', comprising between them no more than around 180,000 individuals, and thus as groups 'doomed to certain extinction'.

The most numerous ethnic group of these is that of the Nenets who, in the same census, were counted at 34,190 persons. Now the Nenets are one of the peoples of Siberia who have best preserved their traditional way of life and culture. The Evenki, almost as numerous (29,901 persons), have on the other hand been subject to considerable assimilation, especially into Yakut groups. Next in order of numerical importance are the Khanty (22,283 persons), then the Eveni (17,055), the Shorians (16,652), the Chukchis (15,107), the Nanai people (11,833), the Koryaks (8,942), the Mansis (8,279), the Dolgans (6,584) and the Nivkhi (4,631). The remaining ethnic groups are undoubtedly 'ultra-minorities':

- The Selkup, the Olchi, the Itelmen and the Udekhe make up between 2,000 and 4,000 people

- The Chuvantsi, the Nganassi, the Yukaghirs, the Kets, the Saami of western Siberia and the Uit of eastern Siberia number between 1,000 and 2,000 people

- Some ethnic groups comprise no more than a few hundred men and women: these are the Orochon people (883 persons), the Karagas people (722), the Aleuts of eastern Siberia (644), the Negidal people (587), the Enets (198) and the Oroki (179)

- One really tiny ethnic group – so small that it was not even counted separately in the census – was that of the Kereks of southern Chukotka, who in total numbered fewer than 50 representatives.

Assimilation of language and of culture has affected all of these small ethnic groups to one extent or another, but so has such assimilation also affected – if less seriously – the more numerously significant groups, such as the Buryats (listed in the census as numbering 417,425 persons), the Yakuts (380,242), the Tuva people (206,160), the Khakass people (78,500) and the Altai people (69,409). Today, just one small proportion of Siberia's original inhabitants preserves an ancient and traditional way of life, continues on a daily basis to practise and to teach its ancestral rituals and language. But such efforts are puny in the face of what is massed against them, notably the effects of 'modern life' and 'technological development' (which include an increased mortality rate, severely depressed morale, stress disorders and diseases, alcoholism, high unemployment, soaring suicides and other measures of progress). It was the frenetic pace at which assimilation was overtaking all these various ethnic groups that caused them to feature in *The Red Book of Ethnic Groups on the Verge of Disappearing*, published during the last years of the Soviet Union.

To understand how this demographic and cultural erosion came about, it is necessary to turn back and look once more at history . . .

COLLISION OF WORLDS

The conquest of Siberia

For a long time blocked by the unwelcome presence of the Tatars, the extension of the Russian Empire on the far side of the Ural Mountains was made possible only on the eventual defeat of the Tatar khan, Kuchum, at the hands of Yermak and his Cossack forces in 1582. The conquest of Siberia was then accomplished at remarkable speed, albeit at the expense of a great deal of blood.

As they continued in their warlike progress ever eastwards, the Cossacks demanded tribute from the populations they overran – tribute not in the form of money but of furs: the yassak. They also constructed forts to control these new subjects of the Russian Tsar . . . and in which to stockpile the precious tribute. Some of the tribespeople, such as the Yakuts, surrendered without much resistance (the Russians were excellent at knowing whom to treat gently and offer gifts to), only to rise in revolt soon afterwards. It was more common, however, for the tribal groups – like the Khanty and the Mansis, the Khakass people, the Evenki and the Eveni people – to act with the utmost ferocity in staving off for as long as possible this hated colonization. The pacification of the north-east of Siberia, from the end of the 17th century, thus took place amid horrifically bloody scenes of combat. The Yukaghirs, and then the Itelmen, sustained heavy losses; whole communities of them were wiped out. The Koryaks kept up their defiant opposition for nigh on 25 years. And only after a full 60 years were the pertinacious Chukchis – a warrior nation – finally subdued, and even then only at the wrong end of the cannons brought in specially by the Russians, forced to adopt unusual methods.

The Tsarist period: colonization and ethnic decline

The incorporation of Siberia into the Russian Empire was accompanied by an influx of colonists and the inauguration of a social system designed to exploit the indigenous populations. The consequences were manifold and immediate: the aboriginal peoples were forcibly suppressed, and made thoroughly aware of their insignificant numeric strength.

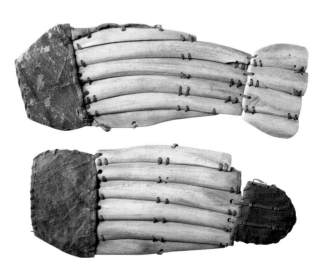

46 Yakut and Eveni children.

47 A warrior's equipment.

48 For the hands of a warrior. Chukchi, the Anadyr area, 1904–1907. Reindeer antler, sealskin, length: i) 36.5 cm, ii) 37 cm.

49 Group of Koryaks beside a *choom*.
Okhotsk, 1896–1897.

50 Eveni Nomads, 1896-1897.

As happened in the Americas, the colonists who came to Siberia brought with them all kinds of viral and bacterial diseases against which the aboriginal peoples had no immunity – smallpox, measles, syphilis among them. Recurrent epidemics racked the defence-less communities. Smallpox alone accounted for the deaths of several thousand Yukaghirs.

The Russians also brought with them new addictions in the form of desirable commodities such as vodka (something else the locals had no immunity against), tobacco, sugar and even bread, which they used in outrageously unequal bartering for the skins and furs so highly sought-after in Europe.

The *yassak* system likewise, over time, was to have repercussions that were all but catastrophic for the peoples of Siberia. Together with the diseases it represented a principal reason for the declining numbers in the population of the ethnic groups during the Tsarist period. So oppressive was the levy of furs that local inhabitants were often forced to go to extreme lengths to get hold of 'the golden pelt'. If the levy had not been fully supplied by the due date, the officers responsible for collecting it had various additional methods of extracting it. One of the more common was to kidnap someone and hold him or her to ransom until it was forthcoming, usually someone important in the community of whoever was defaulting on the tax – perhaps one of the best hunters, a headman, possibly one of the tribal elders. In this way quite often having insufficient time to see to keeping themselves properly fed, exhausted, obliged to do without their leaders or the people most required for the survival of their group, the local people all too frequently underwent periods of famine which, in the environmental conditions natural to the cold north and to Siberia in general, were particularly, insidiously, destructive.

At the beginning of the 18th century, brutality and massacres accompanied the forcible conversion to Christianity of the indigenous peoples. The Russians had realized that 'gentle' methods did not seem to be working. Simultaneously, the colonists continued to exploit the people shamelessly. It was nonetheless only a little later, in 1824, that an official Code of Practice was promulgated by the authorities that was meant to protect the peoples of Siberia from abuses of these kinds. Nothing much came of it.

In the space of two centuries, the conquest and the colonization of Siberia caused a general – in some cases, even permanent – decline in the fortunes of the aboriginal populations. By the end of the 19th century some of the ethnic groups were in such a sorry state (by way of depletion in numbers, wretched health, poverty and low morale) that even then their disappearance altogether was regarded as being only a matter of time – and a short time at that.

The Committee of the North: the hope of renewal

In the early years following the October Revolution, the Soviet authorities took it upon themselves to try to redress the disastrous situation that by then had overtaken most of the peoples of Siberia. A special policy was formulated to protect the ethnic groups that were in the greatest need (of which they listed 26), and, at the initiative of the anthropologist and Chukchi scholar Vladimir Bogoraz (who wrote under the pseudonym N. A. Tan), the Committee of the North was set up to introduce supportive measures. The 'Peoples of the North' were duly exempted from all forms of taxation and from conscription into military service. Some social amenities were placed at the disposal of communities throughout Siberia, each major locality receiving a small schoolhouse, a police station, an infirmary, a veterinarian clinic and a weather station as well as, generally, a small Lenin picture-gallery.

During this early period, some attempt was made to take account of the individual culture of each of the peoples, and the local language. Teaching was in the native tongue and adapted, where necessary, to the nomadic way of life by means of seasonally mobile schools held in wigwams or tent shelters.

51 Pictographic letter. Evenki, Yenisey Province, 1908. Wood (pine), charcoal, length: 59 cm, width: 26 cm.

52 Cross worn on the body. Yakut, 1906. Metal, length: 49 cm.

The Soviet period: the imposition of Communism

The early measures were not in place long enough even to demonstrate how useful they were. Where they were not simply abandoned altogether, they were corrupted into something unrecognizable following the victory of the political radicals who imposed – from that time right up to the end of the Soviet era – their own views of how the indigenous peoples of Siberia were to be transformed, and what they were to become, in order for them to be conformable Soviet citizens.

Accordingly, the collectivization of the means of (food) production began in the 1930s and took ten years or so to be fully applied. The process saw the abrupt confiscation of farming families' livestock, which then became the property of the state and were the responsibility of the large cooperatives, the kolkhozes. Nomadic groups were obliged to settle and become residential, at least outwardly. Those who complained the loudest about collectivization were summarily deported – as on principle were the owners of the largest herds of reindeer. The shamans, around whom native Siberian society pivoted, were outlawed for being mere 'parasites'.

Simultaneously, the standardization of education and the boarding-school system became a highly effective tool in the policy of forced assimilation to the Soviet lifestyle. For the long months of the school year, the children of nomadic groups and from isolated villages were separated from their families and confined in multi-ethnic establishments under the control of Russian-speaking cadres. They were forbidden to speak in their native tongues, and the education they received was different from what they would have learned in their traditional backgrounds. When they came to leave their boarding-schools, each generation of students found itself at odds with parents and relatives, unable to find a place in what had once been home, knowing nothing about the ancestral way of life . . . and incapable of living in the manner best suited to the taiga or the tundra. In the space of just a few years, the precious practical knowledge transmitted from generation to generation for centuries on end was deliberately obliterated.

The increasing marginalization of the aboriginal ethnic groups of Siberia, in the light of the value of the territory's natural resources, could not but reinforce the process of assimilation. From the 1930s, moreover, drawn there by special concessions and benefits, hundreds of thousands, and finally millions, of Soviet migrants flocked into the northern regions where they added to the already abundant manpower within the camps of the Gulags. The flow of migrants actually intensified as the Soviet era came to an end.

During the 1960s, under Nikita Khrushchev, there was a campaign to close the 'little villages with no prospects' which came to a head at the very same time that the local cooperative kolkhozes were redesigned and streamlined as the much larger sovkhozes (state super-farms). Much of the original populations, against their will, were turfed out of their ancestral lands and forcibly relocated in small progressively-minded urban centres otherwise full of Russian-speakers. Those uprooted in this way commonly felt stifled in these new surroundings, but the effect was undoubtedly yet again to speed up the process of 'natural' assimilation – especially as people had to communicate with each other and the TV programmes were all in Russian. Inevitably, intermarriage between Russian-speakers and young people of different ethnic background became fairly widespread.

But there was an even more vexatious consequence of the industrialization of Siberia and the influx into the northern and eastern regions of massive numbers of immigrants: environmental destruction. The list of ruinous effects is long – deforestation in the most easterly zone and on the Pacific coastline; pollution of rivers and lakes (the Ob, the Yenisey, the Vilyuy, Lake Baikal, and so on); acid rain (the High Altai, the area around Lake Baikal); air pollution (Norilsk, the Kuzbass Basin, Magadan, Vladivostok, Khabarovsk); and more. Such forms of pollution of course hit first and hardest the local populations who lived almost exclusively on natural produce in the affected areas. The spoiling of pasturage similarly led to an immedi-

53 A house in the village of Yigansk, on the Lena.

ate reduction in the numbers of livestock and reindeer. Places where the hunting was known to be good suddenly became much smaller – and much emptier once the poachers had got there. Fish became scarce, and those that were caught might often be dangerous to eat.

After Communism, poverty

The economic stagnation which followed the break-up of the Soviet Union bore directly upon the minority groups of the Siberian north. All the advantages they had become accustomed to disappeared overnight, causing a significant downturn in the quality of life. The ethnic communities were suddenly out on their own – seventy years too late. No more motor-fuel, no more helicopters to the rescue and even many of the ordinary social services could no longer be relied on. Healthcare deteriorated to the extent that the mortality rate once more increased sharply, notably through the ravages of (potentially curable) tuberculosis. Living conditions in the north became severe – so much so that women were no longer willing to accompany men into the taiga, far less the tundra, and the number of marriages plummeted, as did the birth rate correspondingly.

The loss of a sense of tradition, the uprooting of cultural identity, uncertainty over the future and overall poverty are factors easily understood as leading towards self-destructive tendencies which, in this case, often translated into an addiction to alcohol. In the villages of the north, therefore, one commodity that is never likely to run out is vodka, even though its price rises steeply at night-time and on pay-days. The suicide rate has soared, and fatal accidents linked in one way or another with drunkenness are now nothing out of the ordinary. Indeed, life expectancy for ethnic peoples in Siberia – less than 50 years for men – is the lowest in all of Russia.

The will to live: renewal

This sombre picture nonetheless contains a tiny speck of optimism subsumed in the single word *renewal*. Since the 1970s, many of the different communities in Siberia have discovered among themselves writers, poets and artists, all intimately concerned with the catastrophic fate of their fellow aboriginals, and all refusing to admit even the possibility of their own ancestral culture's extinction. They include people whose names are today well known, such as Vladimir Sanghi (of the Nivkhi), Yuri Rytkhe (Chukchi), Anna Nerkagi (Nenets), and the Kurilov brothers (Yukaghirs).

At the advent of *Perestroika*, such concerns bubbled to the surface and began to be expressed forthrightly, to cause people to come together to talk and to take action. It may have started among what passed for the elite, but it was soon very much the preoccupation of large sections of the whole populace. A movement for the renewal, the renaissance, of the peoples of Siberia had been born, embodied by the Association for the Minority Peoples of the North, formally founded in 1989. This association contains members representing all the minority groups of Siberia, from the far north to the extreme east of 'Russian' Asia, dedicated to defending the rights of the aboriginal communities, to the protection of their ancestral lands, to the furtherance of independence, to the preservation of the ethnic cultures, traditions and languages, to freedom to choose their preferred way of life. The precepts of the association are relayed throughout Siberia by a network of branches and local groups of all kinds, including folklore societies and cultural arts and crafts clubs, whose task requires considerable effort and perseverance. For many, the aim seems to be forever just out of reach, as the rehabilitation of ancestral practices would seem to depend as much on local economics. The larger ethnic groups in Siberia, such as the Yakuts and the Buryats, after all, are finding renewal – renaissance – much easier because they are generally far better organized and have their own standing institutions that benefit from an annual budget intended specifically to cater for matters of cultural heritage. (These ethnic groups are the subject of special clauses within the constitution of the local 'Autonomous' Republic of the Russian Federation, and have been now for 20 years.)

*

The realities of life for the peoples of the north today are far from simple. A good third of the aboriginal populations have become entirely urbanized and are no longer distinguishable from other members of the public. The remainder live as best they can in their rural surroundings, perhaps half-engaged in traditional activities, perhaps half doing other things or simply unemployed.

For all the pain of assimilation, and for all the traditional ancestral practices with which the younger generation has failed to become familiar, the essential contribution bequeathed to the world by the ethnic cultures of Siberia seems, nonetheless, in general, being maintained. That contribution is made up of a way of life founded directly on closeness to and dependence on nature, and on a holistic vision of the world and of humankind's place in it, both recognizable even now in the persistence of animist rituals (or less often, shamanist rituals).

The next section of this book makes contact with such original ways of life, original ways of thinking – original, that is, in the sense both of being primeval and unlike anything else – so characteristic of the aboriginal peoples of Siberia.

54 Reindeer-herders listening to a radio. Chukchis, Magadan, 1970s.

THE TRADITIONAL WAY OF LIFE IN SIBERIAN COMMUNITIES

LIFESTYLES IN SIBERIA

The traditional lifestyles of the various communities that live in Siberia depend on one or more activities – fishing, hunting, the herding of reindeer or the breeding of cattle – that are specific to their locality, but also subject to regional variations, some of them significant, even within a single ethnic group. So, for example, the Evenki may herd reindeer and hunt, may hunt and fish, or may instead farm cattle and breed horses depending on where they live. The Eveni people, on the other hand, herd reindeer and go hunting in the tundra and the taiga, while on the shores of the Sea of Okhotsk they rely solely on catching marine creatures.

Communities in Siberia tend by tradition to live on the resources available to them, making the best of the geographical and climatic conditions. Factors that have a far-reaching influence on their everyday lives include fragile ecosystems; the long cold, dark, northern winter; the migration of herds; the hibernation of some of their food species; the brevity of the crop-growing period.

Reindeer herders thus take it for granted that when the reindeer make their annual move to seek out new pasturage, they must go with them, so becoming nomads. The arrival in the far north of migrant birds in May marks the beginning of the most bountiful hunting season of the year. In spring and autumn various species of fish swim up the rivers to spawn. Each has its own preferred riverine destination – salmon, for instance, find their way far upriver to the shallow headstreams. And the fishermen naturally follow season after season to where their preferred fish are most plentiful, to make their best catches while the fish are at their meatiest and while the females are full of roe. In summer the brief period of plant growth is punctuated by the ripening of different types of berry, one after the other, in their preferred surroundings.

At the coasts, however, there are always animals and birds to catch, which means that littoral communities have through the millennia never needed to become nomadic.

55 Chukchi reindeer-herder in traditional costume. 1970s.

The fauna and the flora, the regenerative cycle of nature in Siberia – all determine the rhythm of life of the aboriginal people, and embody an annual calendar of things to do and things to go and get for individual groups and, indeed, for individual individuals.

The peoples of Siberia are the inheritors of highly practical and specific traditions that distinguish one group from another but yet contain elements common to all. Take food, for example. Just about all the inhabitants of Siberia eat fish, although it is prepared in various fashions. The most widespread recipe – known from north to south and from east to west – is undoubtedly *yukola*, in which the fish is dried on large wooden frames in the summer sun to preserve it for the winter. Highly nourishing, the *yukola* has for centuries taken on the same role for Siberian groups that bread plays elsewhere in the world. Similarly, *stroganina* is the dish of choice for inhabitants of some of the coldest regions: it is fish caught in winter and frozen the instant it leaves the water in air temperatures of under –40°C (-72°F), preserved, and eaten just as it is, cut into fine strips. A favourite of all dwellers in the north, Russians as well as indigenous peoples, *stroganina* is mostly kept for special occasions. In the smaller villages, the fish may be stored frozen on the outdoor porches and balconies of the houses over the winter (for the average temperature outside is usually lower than that of electric freezers anyway).

56 Yakut summer encampment at haymaking time.

57 Eveni woman's costume, seen from the back. Reindeer fur, cured reindeer-hide, sealskin, ground squirrel.

58 An Eveni woman's clothes.

59 Evenki man's clothing. Okhotsk area, 1904. Horse-hide, reindeer hair, glass beads, cured hide (leather), linen. Tunic length: 90 cm; length of the chest decoration: 89 cm; length of the feet: 28 cm. Width of the chest decoration: 49 cm. Height of the boots: 36 cm.

60 Pair of trousers for a man. Evenki, Yenisey Province, 1908. Cured hide (leather), glass beads, cotton fabric, reindeer hide, length: 38 cm.

61 Outside covering for a haversack. Evenki, Okhotsk area, 1905. Reindeer fur, linen, cotton velvet, glass beads, length: 61 cm, width: 38 cm.

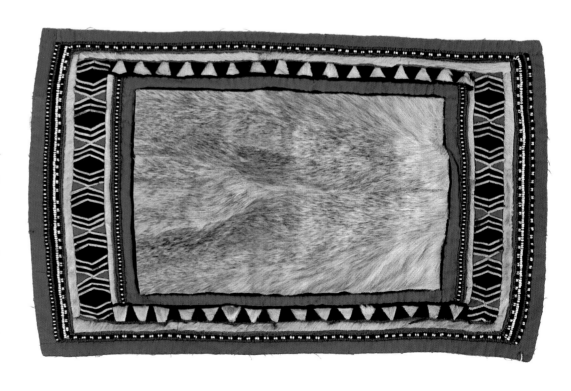

62 Wall-hanging, possibly based on a
Russian original. Markovo village,
Kamchatka, 1910. Reindeer-hide,
length: 236 cm, width: 291 cm.

63 Seasonal nomadism among the
Evenki. Yenisey Province, beginning of
the 20th century.

64 Woman tanning a reindeer-hide inside a *yarang*. Chukchi, Amguema village, 1987.

65 Girdle for an Evenki woman. Lower Tunguska Basin, beginning of the 20th century. Cured hide (leather), glass beads, pearls, metal, length: 91 cm, width: 9 cm.

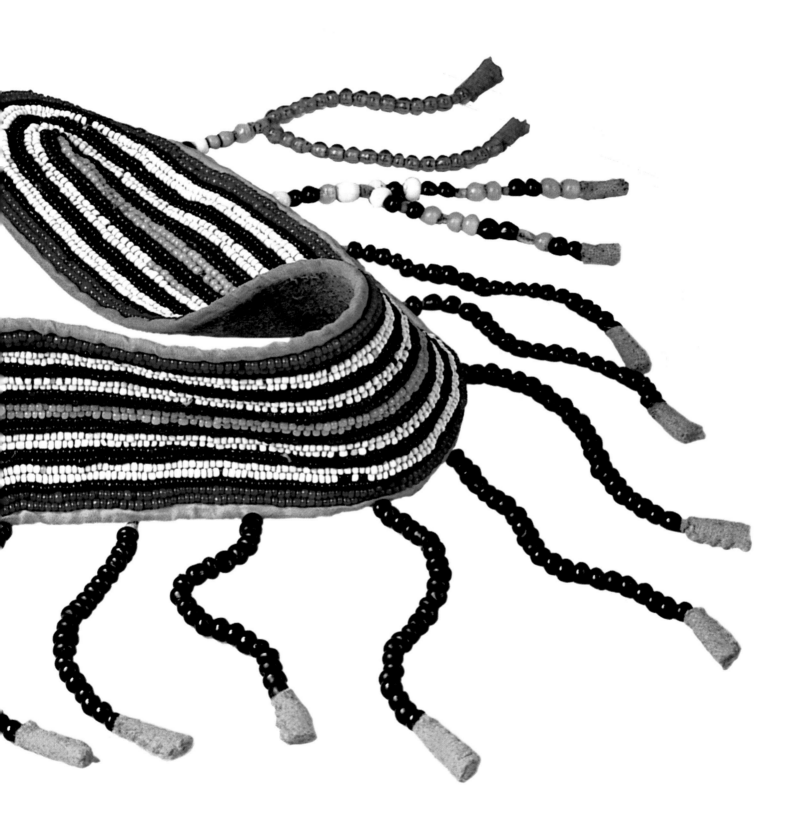

Another constant among the differing traditions is the use of natural materials – wood, bark, furs and skins – to make clothing, handicraft-work and/or a shelter. Throughout all the regions of Siberia, reindeer-skin is most used for winter clothing, in particular for knee-boots fashioned from strips of hide taken from the lower limbs of the reindeer. The more northerly peoples – the Nenets, Nganassani, Yukaghirs, Chukchis, and so forth – tend to make their shoes and boots from the little piece of roughened skin that lies between the large and the small parts of the hoof of the reindeer. Although an inordinate quantity of such pieces is required for even one pair, the resultant shoes are guaranteed to keep the feet warm and dry.

The traditional lifestyles of the peoples of Siberia, many aspects of which have in recent times changed or indeed been lost altogether, have one other thing in common: the ability to adapt to a hostile environment. Such practical knowledge, vital to these northern ethnic groups, represents a heritage that ought to be precious to all humankind – knowledge of northern environments, of the flora and fauna there, of the climate; knowledge, gained over thousand of years and handed down from generation to generation, that not only enables people to survive in such conditions but that also represents an expression of their artistic creativity.

66 Carved miniature: 'Voyage on reindeer-back'. Chukchi, Anadyr area, 1906. Walrus ivory, length 7.5 cm, max. height: 7 cm.

67 Representation of a woman. Koryak, Anadyr area, 1906. Reindeer antler, height: 10.7 cm.

68 'Working with skins'. Chukchi, Koryak, Chukchi Peninsula and Kamchatka, end of the 19th and beginning of the 20th century.

Following the reindeer

It was the Evenki and the Eveni people who made the first attempt at domesticating the reindeer, which even now they use as a form of transport particularly well adapted to the region of the taiga, especially in hunting other ungulates. The reindeer is the focus round which the world revolves for these two communities, who often call themselves in their own languages 'the people of the reindeer'.

An activity typical of Siberia, reindeer-herding is practised – more or less intensively – by ten ethnic groups: the Nenets, the Nganassani people, the Chukchis, the Koryaks, the Evenki, the Eveni, the Dolgans, the Yukaghirs, the Khanty and the Karagas people. Methodologies differ in the tundra and the taiga.

In the taiga, herds are comparatively small, averaging between 20 and 25 head, with perhaps 50 head in the largest herds. Here, the reindeer is used primarily as a means of transport, the people for the most part living by hunting and fishing. The Khanty, for example, herd reindeer (which in fact was something they copied from the Nenets) only as a sideline. Reindeer are credited with more importance in the tundra, where herds are larger and of variable size – from a hundred or so to several thousand head. The semi-domesticated reindeer represents an essential source of livelihood for the peoples of the far north.

Lichens and mosses, the main diet of the reindeer, tend only to grow some 3 millimetres (an eighth of an inch) per year. When all have been consumed in an area, the reindeer have to leave and find new pasturage. This seasonal migration of the reindeer is naturally reflected in the life of their herders and those who go hunting with them. The journeys involved in the migrations are proportional to the overall size of the herds, for the more head of reindeer there are in a herd, the more important it is to find a large area of fresh lichens and mosses (from the taiga or the intermediate zone between taiga and tundra in the wintertime – where the reindeer can more easily find their food under the snow and the men can find firewood to keep themselves warm – to the vast bare expanses of the north in summertime). Small herds, in tundra or taiga, tend to cover short distances when travelling from summer to winter pastures – an average of perhaps 25 to 37 miles (40 to 60 kilometres), 60 miles (100 kilometres) at the most. In the taiga, the reindeer-herders who use reindeer for hunting select migratory paths that accord with migratory patterns of the animals they want to hunt or with places known to be the habitat of the fish they want to catch.

69 Reindeer-herders in the tundra.
Chukchi, Anadyr area, 1979.

70 Reindeer plaything. Koryak,
Kamchatka, 1897. Wood, length:
18 cm, height: 12 cm.

71 Doll-woman. Evenki, Yenisey
Province, 1907. Cloth, reindeer-bone
and -fur, glass beads, length: 11 cm.

In western Siberia, the largest of the reindeer-herders are the Nenets; in the east the Chukchis and the Koryaks. Less well organized than the Nenets, the 'Chaochus' and the 'Chavchuven' (which is what the Chukchi and Koryak reindeer bosses call themselves) keep the numerically most prolific herds in the whole of Siberia. The Nenets tend to the grazing of the reindeer all the year round: the herds are kept under observation day after day by herdsmen with the help of dogs trained to round up any stray animals. With the Chukchis and the Koryaks, at least until the 1950s, the herd was left to its own devices once it reached pasturage, with the result that the herdsmen – who had no dogs – often had to spend a considerable time rounding up stray reindeer.

The reindeer of the Eveni people are regarded as particularly valuable by the Chukchis and the Koryaks, who were once willing to exchange two of their own animals for one of the Eveni's. It was the same in respect of all the reindeer of the taiga, highly appreciated for their larger overall size by the herders of the tundra.

The tundra herders do not ride their animals but harness them to sledges (sleighs) for the transportation of goods and passengers. In the taiga, riding reindeer is the primary means of transport for the Evenki and the Eveni. The reindeer makes an excellent mount in wooded and mountainous terrain, as the Tuva people – who breed cattle and horses down in the south of Siberia – can attest, for they too use them to get around in their mountains.

Reindeer-herding is a testing business physically, and not just in winter, because of hunger and cold. After the fawning season (which takes place in May), the herdsmen have to watch day and night over the young fawns to make sure they are not snatched by wolves. Towards the end of summer, when the wild mushrooms pop up all over the place, they have to be even more vigilant, for reindeer adore such potentially harmful delicacies. And so, for their own health and security, the herd of animals has gradually to be more restricted, until they are penned every night (the Arctic day is already coming to its end) in an enclosure next to the encampment.

72 Child's overalls. Koryak. Reindeer-hide and cured hide (leather).

73 Child's doll. Koryak. Reindeer-hide, beadwork.

74 Doll-woman. Eveni, Anadyr area,
1910. Reindeer-hide, linen, cotton,
glass beads, cured hide (leather),
height: 16 cm.

The diet of the herders of the taiga for the most part comprises items they have hunted, caught (in the form of fish) or gathered (in the form of berries and fungi). The proprietors of the largest reindeer herds, on the other hand, live almost entirely on the resources provided by their own animals, beginning with the slaughter of one of the herd at the beginning of the autumn. Every bit of the reindeer has its own use: nothing at all goes to waste. The meat is eaten boiled, raw or frozen. To preserve it, it may be smoked. The blood is drunk still lukewarm from the slaughter, and the raw marrow is regarded as the herdsmen's treat. The fat is usually eaten with the meat but may alternatively be used to provide lighting – the Nenets make candles out of it. From the tendons and sinews comes a thread useful in making clothes and as string or cord. The skin can be plied into thongs and then turned into a lasso, into straps or reins for the harnesses or into bridles. The furry parts of the skin of the reindeer are ordinarily used to fashion garments or to make up the huge, heavy carpet-coverings that insulate the tent- or wigwam-like dwellings of the nomadic hunter-herders.

Such dwellings come in two varieties. The Nenets, the Nganassani people, the Dolgans, the Evenki and some others in central and western Siberia make use of what they call a *choom*, whereas the peoples to the north and east of them – the Chukchis, Koryaks, Eveni – make their temporary home in a *yarang*.

The *choom*, which is conical in shape, is a sort of movable wigwam set up around a framework of between 20 and 50 poles stuck in the ground in a circle and tied together at the top. In the winter this framework is covered with two layers of reindeer-hide, furry sides out, so that the interior of the *choom* is lined with fur and the outside also presents fur to the elements, and there is a minimal insulation space between the two. In summertime, instead of the skins, the *choom* is tightly encased in strips of birch-bark or densely-packed moss. The open area in the middle of the *choom* is occupied by two horizontal poles some 5 feet (1.5 metres) or so off the ground, from which all kinds of things can be suspended over the fire – urns, cauldrons, billycans, clothing, footwear and just about anything else. For the Nenets, the living space in the *choom* is to the left and right of the entrance, each side of the hearth. On the ground, the floor is strewn with willow stems and dry grass and carpeted with reindeer skin. The side of the choom opposite the entrance is the area that has to be kept 'pure' and clean at all times, for this is where the family's sacred objects are located, together with the cooking and eating vessels and the food stocks. For the Evenki, the side either to the right or to the left of the entrance is reserved for women, the central area is reserved for other members of the family, and the back – opposite the entrance – is for male guests.

The *yarang* is rather different, though still wigwam-like. It is cylindrical from the ground up but tapers to a cone at the top – a shape that is particularly effective in withstanding squalls and Arctic storms. During winter the framework of poles is hung around with reindeer hides that are held down with heavy stones or with sledges pegged into the snow. The entrance to the *yarang* is traditionally to the east or north-east. Putting it up and taking it down, collecting and packing up all its bits and pieces (the coverings, hangings, carpets, poles and the rest) ready for moving is a job for the women. Among the Koryaks and the Chukchis, an encampment comprises between five and ten *yarangs*, each accommodating one or two families who are blood-relations or are related by marriage. It takes around twenty sledges to move one *yarang* and its complement of occupants. The largest of the reindeer-herders in former times, some of whom owned up to 5,000 reindeer, might need 150 sledges.

75 Chukchi encampment. Kamchatka,
1912.

76 Pastor and reindeer-herder. Koryak, Kamchatka Peninsula, end of the 19th and beginning of the 20th century.

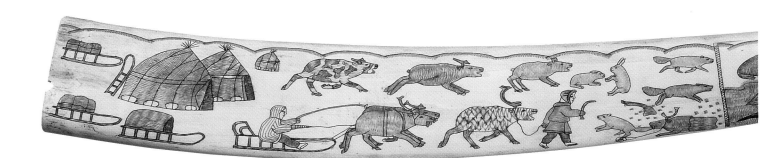

Reindeer fur is beautifully warm, which of course is why it is utilized so much by the aboriginal peoples of Siberia not only as an insulating covering for the ground and for the linings of the *chooms* and *yarangs*, but also in the making of clothing – especially clothing for the reindeer herdsmen and the hunters who are required to spend considerable periods of time out of doors during the winter.

The Nenets wear the *malitsa*, a large reindeer-fur tunic with an integral hood and mittens – the fur on the inside. When it becomes really cold, they put on, over the *malitsa*, another garment made of reindeer-hide called the *sokwi*, which has its own hood. The *sokwi* of the Nenets and the Nganassani hunters is stitched together from different materials: from reindeer-skin at the back in order to keep the shoulders and lumbar region warm, and from dog-skin at the front in order to soundproof the movements of the hunters as they go.

The Chukchis and the Koryaks wear the *kukhlianka*, a reindeer-fur double tunic – double because it is made in two pieces so that there is fur on the inside *and* on the outside. The neck and the sleeves of the *kukhlianka* are sometimes decorated with strips of dog- or wolverine-fur.

Reindeer-skin snow-boots (*untiy*, *torbaza*, and other technical terms), ornamented with glass beads on the front and most often with a felt sole, are worn in all the regions of northern Siberia, even in the towns.

The skin of the semi-domesticated reindeer varies from snow-white to dark grey or nut-brown. A brown skin with white spots is most sought-after for making festive clothes, which differ from ordinary everyday clothes in that they tend to be covered in metal ornaments and/or strands of multicoloured glass beads, or to be hung about with all kind of pendants (for instance, little furry animals dressed in the ethnic costume of the Eveni people).

From the month of April, the inhabitants of the tundra and the taiga have to shield their eyes against the reflection of the sun on the snow and against the wind. In the past they used to use special eyeshades split into two sections horizontally, made in metal, birch-bark or wood, or otherwise just lengths of coarse hair.

77 Carved walrus tusk, in colour (secondary face). Fragment, Chukchi, Chukchi Peninsula, 1930s. Walrus ivory, length: 62 cm, width: 6 cm.

78 Woman's knife for cutting up meat, for shaping hides and furs, or (in former times) for cutting the umbilical cord of the new-born. Chukchi, beginning of the 20th century. Metal, walrus ivory, length: 20 cm, handle length: 11 cm.

79 Carved miniature: 'Tea time' and 'Trapeze'. Koryak, Kamchatka Peninsula, 1911. Walrus ivory, length: i) 6 cm, ii) 6.7 cm, height: i) 4.5 cm, ii) 7 cm.

80 An old man's clothing. Chukchi, 1904–1907.

81 An old man's clothing. Chukchi, 1904–1907.

82 Girl's tunic, seen from the back. Evenki, Yenisey Province, 1905. Cured hide (leather), horsehair, glass beads, pearls, length: 88 cm.

83 Evenki girl's costume. Yenisey Province, around 1905. Cured hide (leather), horsehair, glass beads, pearls, reindeer fur, cotton fabric. Tunic length: 88 cm, length of the decoration on the front: 90 cm, width: 38 cm.

84 Children near a *choom*. Yenisey
Province, beginning of the 20th
century.

85 Evenki people beside a *choom* in summer. Okhotsk region.

86 Man's winter clothing. Koryak, 1970s. Reindeer-hide, dog-skin, cured hide (leather), glass beads. Length of *kukhlianka*: 126 cm, length of trousers: 106 and 110 cm, length of footwear: 71 and 74 cm, length of soles: 32 and 31 cm; height of *chapka*: 32 cm, width of *chapka*: 33 cm.

87 Woman's winter clothing. Chukchi, Chukchi Peninsula, 1970s. Reindeer-hide, dog-skin, cured hide (leather), length: 103 cm.

88 Woman's festive clothing. Koryak, Kamchatka, 1970s. Reindeer-hide, dog-skin, cured reindeer-skin, glass beads. Length of *kukhlianka*: 127 cm, length of sleeves: 130 cm, length of footwear: 26 cm, height of boots: 28 cm.

89 Woman's festive clothing. Yakut, 1903, 1908. Linen, brocade, the furs of beaver, otter, ground squirrel, wolverine, sable and lynx, metal, silk, other fabrics, pearls. Length of pelisse: 134 cm, length of *chapka*: 70 cm, length of head ornament: 97 cm.

90 Hunter performing a ritual over a
slain bear. Evenki, Yenisey Province,
beginning of the 20th century.

COASTAL PEOPLES: HUNTERS OF MARINE MAMMALS

On the shores of the Arctic and the Pacific Oceans, some nomadic or semi-nomadic groups tend to hunt marine mammals (occasionally even in the summer) for their skins, their fat or just for a change of meat in the daily diet. Such groups include the Nenets – should they happen to travel as far north as the Arctic coast during their seasonal summer migration – and the Nganassani people, and on the Pacific coast the Evenki, the Olchi, the Oroki and the Orochon people. For the Nivkhi people of Sakhalin island and especially in the extreme north-east for the Aleuts, the Uit (Eskimos) and for the coastal groups of Chukchis (the *Ankaliniy*), of Koryaks (the *Nymylany*) and of Evenei (the *Nemeh*), the hunting of marine mammals is the basis of their way of life, the foundation of their traditional culture in a temporal and spiritual sense.

The Bering Strait, the shores of the bay at Lavrentiya and the environs of Novoye Chaplino are locations where the hunting of marine mammals is a speciality. In this area (on the Chukotskiy Peninsula), the villages of the hunters follow the coastline, winding in with the bays and out with the promontories. From their own houses the hunters have a full view of the sea, and may even be able to mark down individual animals that would make suitable targets: walruses, seals, belugas and whales.

The traditional weapons for the hunt are the harpoon and the spear, long replaced now, of course, by the rifle. The techniques and traditional methods of hunting, which are numerous, differ according to the season, to the animal that is the quarry – and to the ancestral beliefs about that animal.

91 Baskets. Aleut, Koryak, Commander Islands, Kamchatka Peninsula, beginning of the 20th century. Seaweed, pearls, fur, paint, cured hide (leather). Diameter: i) 25.5 cm, top diameter: 17.2 cm; ii) base diameter: 22 cm; height: i) 12 cm, ii) 13 cm.

92 Baskets. Aleut, Aleutian Islands, Umnak island, 1909–1910. Seaweed, fur, base diameter: i) 11.5 cm, ii) 18 cm, iii) 32.5 cm.

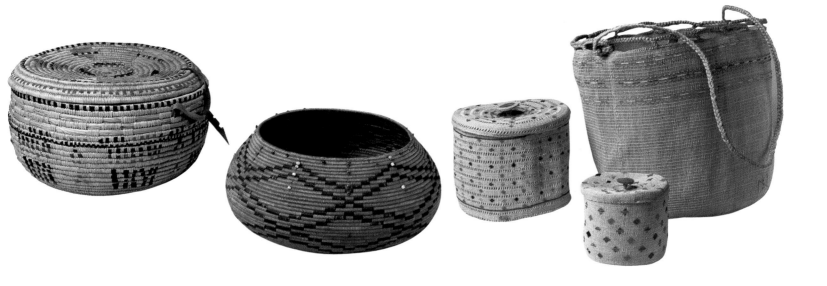

The beginning of winter, while the ice is still fairly thin, is the time to catch seals, using baited lines lowered through the top of the ice-floe where an animal has made a hole through which to breathe. The same technique is employed in catching fur-seals. What usually happens is that the hunter remains completely motionless next to the hole, facing the wind, waiting for the creature to emerge. As soon as it does, he gaffs it with his harpoon, and kills it with a rifle shot. Among the Chukchis, dogs are specially trained to sniff out the breathing-holes.

At the beginning of spring, when the seals take to basking in the sunshine on top of the ice-floes, the hunters get as close as they can to them by humping along on their stomachs, mimicking the awkward movements and even the sounds of the animals themselves, sometimes also assisted by being camouflaged with sealskin.

For the Aleuts and the Eskimos the hunting season begins when the ice melts and they take to sea in their kayaks. The Chukchis and the Koryaks do the same in their bidarkas. Both types of boat are of variable length but particularly light and strong, made as they are of flexible sealskin or walrus-skin stretched over a wooden frame.

93 Carved walrus tusk, in colour (primary face). Chukchi, Chukchi Peninsula, 1930s. Walrus ivory, length: 51 cm, width: 7 cm

94 Spoon. Aleut, north-west Alaska, beginning of the 20th century. Wood, length: 28.5 cm.

95 Carved walrus tusk. Chukchi.

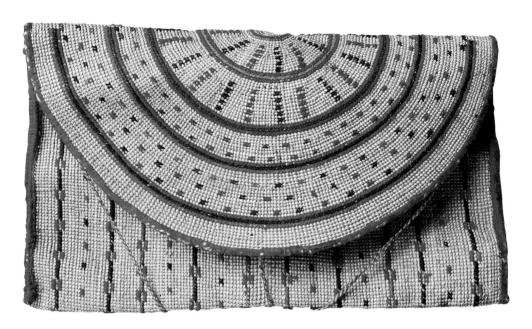

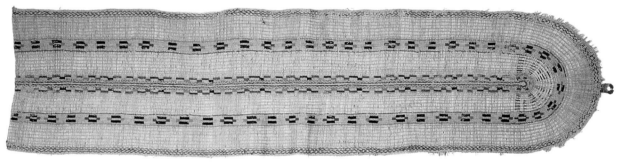

96 Satchel belonging to an Aleut woman. Seaweed, fur, fabric.

97 Woman's cape. Aleut, Aleutian Islands, Umnak island, 1912. Seaweed, hide, length: 74 cm, width: at top 46 cm, at bottom 181 cm.birdskin. Length: 34 cm, width: 36 cm.

98 Small rug. Aleut, Aleutian Islands, 1909–1910. Seaweed, fur, hide, length: 155 cm, width: 39 cm.

99 Scrimshaw: 'Rorqual with a seal in its mouth'. Eskimo (Uit), Chukotka, beginning of the 20th century. Walrus ivory, length: 7.5 cm, height: 2.7 cm.

100 Carved ministure: 'Seal hunt'. Chukchi, 1906. Walrus ivory, length: 17.8 cm, max. height: 2.8 cm.

101 Carved walrus tusk. Chukchi.

102 Carved walrus tusk, in colour (secondary face). Fragment, Chukchi, Chukchi Peninsula, 1930s. Walrus ivory, length: 57 cm, width: 6 cm.

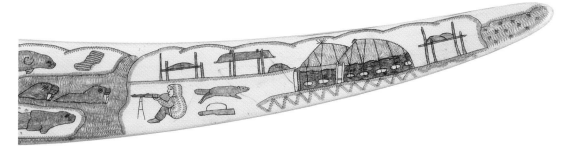

103 Eskimo with a whaling harpoon.
Chaplino village, Chukchi Peninsula,
1953

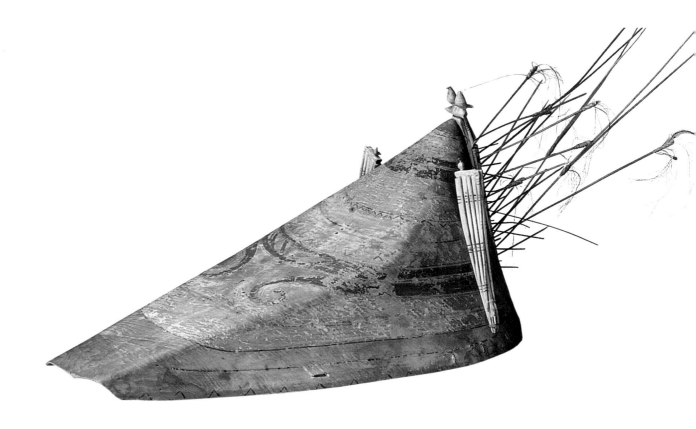

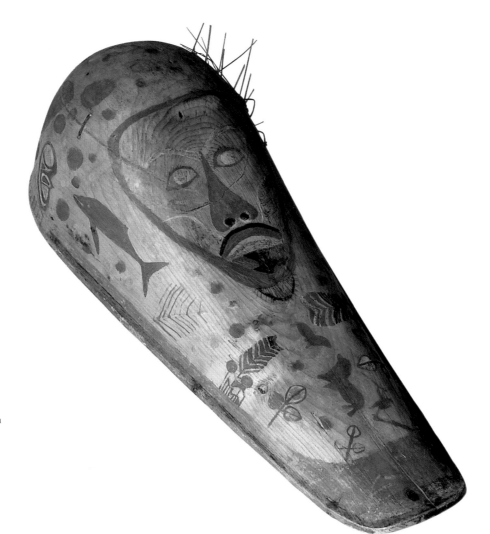

104 Hunter's headgear. Aleut, Aleutian
Islands, beginning of the 20th century.
Wood, bone, hair, length: 38.5 cm,
height: 22 cm.

105 Hunter's headgear. Aleut,
Commander Islands, beginning of the
20th century. Wood, length: 54 cm,
height: 17 cm.

Catching seals may be something that can be done by one person, but catching walruses or whales has to be a group activity and with several bidarkas. Each bidarka is occupied by a crew of between six and ten men – one or two with harpoons at the prow, five or six oarsmen in the body of the boat, and on the rudder at the stern the owner of the bidarka. Once a walrus is spotted, the oarsmen hastily propel the boat towards the creature, and the men at the prow hurl their harpoons, which are attached to their belts by a long cord. If the point of one or both harpoons is firmly fixed in the body of the walrus, the cord attached drags on the creature, preventing its movement and tiring it, allowing the hunters to close in. It is finally despatched, either with a spear or, more often now, by rifle shot. Back on dry land, the corpse is cut up and its flesh shared out in an equitable manner between all the members of the community.

Much the same techniques are used when hunting the whale, but of course many more bidarkas are required (for the animal is that much bigger). The capture of a whale is cause for great celebration, for just one of these mammals provides enough food and other resources for an entire village for a year. The bounty of the sea thus bestows indispensable gifts on the coastal populations: things to eat, things to burn and things for the household (including materials for handicrafts and clothing).

The hunters of marine creatures lay up their bidarkas over the winter, and their sledges over the summer, on solid supports some 6foot 6inches (2metres) or so high. In the past, these supports were whale ribs driven into the ground. Whale ribs and jawbones also used once to form the rounded framework of the traditional dwellings of the coastal communities in the north-east of Siberia – the ancient half-buried lodges covered over with earth and moss. Among the Uit such lodges could shelter an entire community of some 40 people. Among the Chukchis and the Koryaks, the entrance to a half-buried lodge like this in summer was through an opening in the roof leading to a ladder carved from the trunk of a tree. In winter, in order to maintain the warmth inside the lodge, entry was via a long passage that started at ground-level. Seal skins were used as floor-carpeting and/or to cover the walls of the dwelling. For light and heat, moss was burned with whale fat or walrus fat on a hearth made of stone or fireclay. This setup also facilitated the cooking of food. Fat was evidently a particularly precious, if not indispensable, substance – the Eskimos used to keep it in containers made out of the bladders of whales or walruses, the Chukchis in sealskin pouches – for it could also be used as a bartering medium to obtain furs or reindeer meat from passing nomads.

Today, only the dilapidated ruins of such lodges remain, abandoned now for nigh on 150 years in favour of the *yarang* or of wooden houses. Inside the *yarangs*, candles have replaced the whale-oil lamps.

By tradition, summer clothing was always made of the skins (or various internal parts) of seals, walruses or bears, whereas winter clothing was made of reindeer-hide. Before they began to barter with the reindeer-herders, however, the Eskimos also used the skins and feathers of birds in their clothing. Today they wear fur socks and stockings, over which are knee-boots and trousers made of sealskin with the fur on the inside. In extremely cold conditions, like the Chukchis and Koryaks they wear the reindeer-skin *kukhlianka*. On top of all other clothing they can wear the *kamleyka*, a garment stitched together with the completely waterproof intestinal membrane of the walrus: it is particularly commonly used for hunting trips at sea where its remarkable waterproof and humidity-proof qualities are especially appreciated.

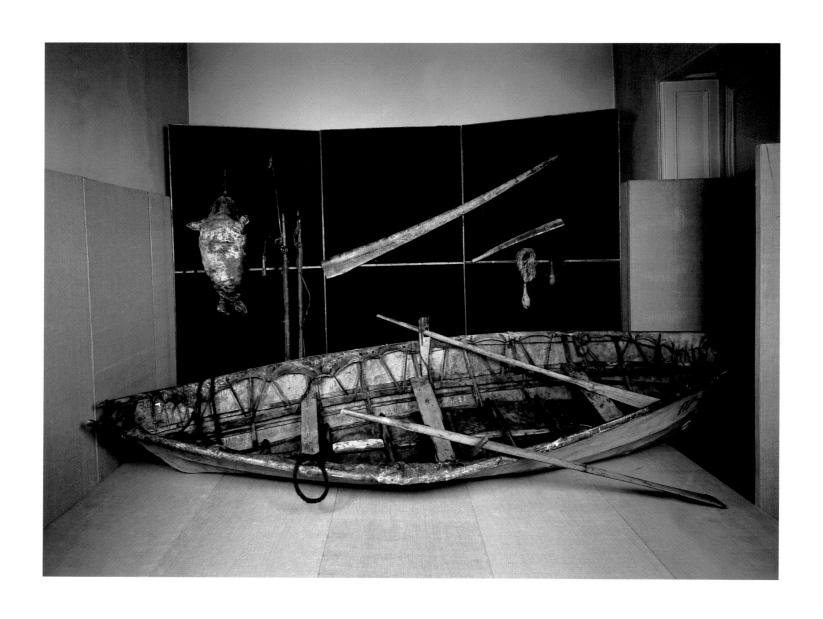

106 Bidarka, equipment and weapons for a communal offshore hunting expedition. Chukchi, Eskimo (Uit), 1970–1974.

107 Figurine: 'Hunter in a bidarka'. Eskimo (Uit), beginning of the 20th century. Wood, length: 46 cm, height: 8.5 cm.

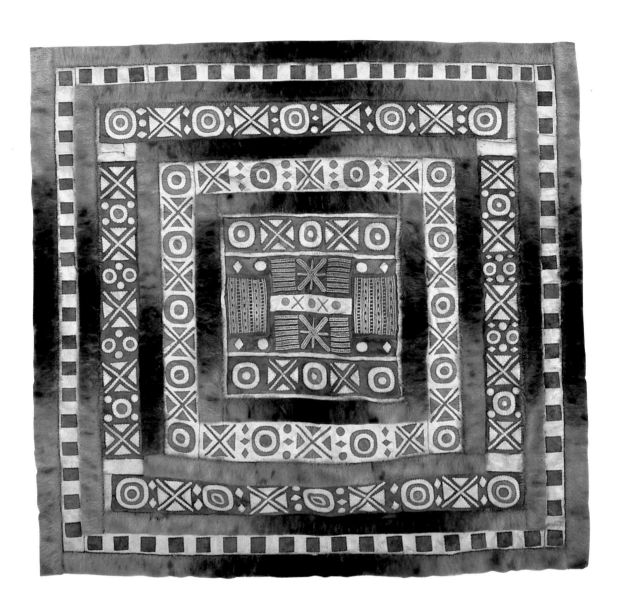

108 Small rug. Eskimo (Uit), Kamchatka, 1909. Sealskin and -fur, stitching in reindeer-hide, length: 70 cm, width: 68.5 cm.

109 Hunter's lucky charm. Aleut, Aleutian Islands. Wood, skin, walrus ivory, lower diameter: 29.8–21.8 cm, height: 8.7 cm.

110 Woman's bag. Eskimo (Uit),
Chukchi Peninsula, beginning of the
20th century. Sealskin and -fur,
stitching in reindeer-hide, length:
37 cm, width: 49 cm.

111 Woman's bag. Aleut, Aleutian
Islands, 1909–1910. Intestinal
membranes of sea creatures, down
(bird's feathers), fur,

112 The cutting up of a walrus.
Chukchi shore residents, Magadan,
1953.

113 Cutting up a whale after a sea-hunt. Chukchi, Eskimo (Uit).

In the diet of these coastal dwellers, the meat and fat of marine mammals not unnaturally occupies a dominant position. The meat is eaten raw, smoked, boiled, frozen or even in a state of fermentation. To preserve walrus or whale meat for the winter, the Chukchis get it to ferment by hermetically enclosing it inside a seal-skin pouch and burying it in the summertime in a place that remains covered in snow all year. In this way they assure themselves of a supply of fermented meat in winter that has also been kept naturally frozen in the permafrost. The blackened and stringy skin of the whale, with its fine layers of pinkish fat, is a real treat for hunters of sea creatures.

The food of the coastal peoples also includes reindeer meat, fish (from which they make *yukola*), berries and the occasional vegetable.

Finally, the bones. The tusks of the walrus and the ribs and jawbones of the whale now principally serve to supply the medium for a form of art that has reached a surprisingly high standard. All the coastal peoples have long practised it, and are expert at it. It is the carving of statuettes – of people or of animals, of hunting scenes or of scenes of family and social life – in 'marine' ivory. These solid down-to-earth representations in tusk and bone are at the same time representations of the internal world of the dwellers of the far north.

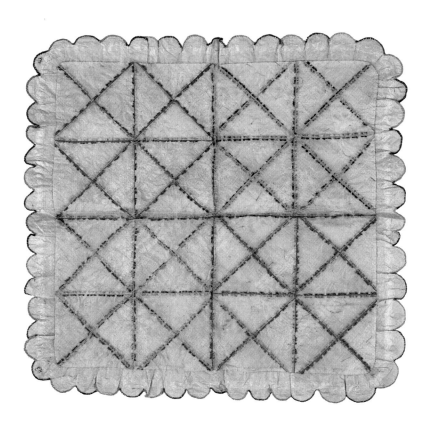

114 Footwear for a man. Eskimo (Uit), Alaska, beginning of the 20th century. Sealskin, walrus-skin, length of the sole: 27 cm, height: 19 cm.

115 Small rug. Aleut, Aleutian Islands, 1909–1910. Intestinal membranes of sea creatures, fabric, down (bird's feathers), fur. Length: 33 cm, width: 28 cm.

116 Drying out walrus-skins.
Chukchi, Eskimo (Uit).

117 Oil lamp for heating and lighting. Chukchi, Anadyr area, beginning of the 20th century. Stone, diameter: 16 cm, height: 7 cm.

118 Rug. Eskimo (Uit), Chukchi Peninsula, 1926. Sealskin, reindeer-hide, fur, diameter: 95 cm.

119 Carved miniature: 'The bear hunt'. 1906. Walrus ivory, height: 14 cm, width: 5.7 cm.

120 Small scraper for cleaning the intestines of sea creatures. Eskimo (Uit). Walrus ivory and wood.

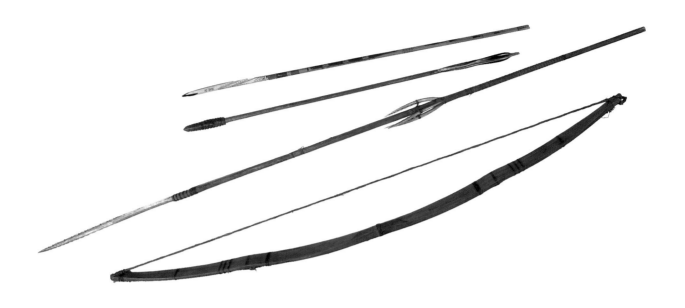

121 Bow and arrows for hunting marine mammals. End of the 19th, beginning of the 20th century. Wood, bone, tendons, feathers.

122 Arrow. Fragment, Aleut, north-east Alaska, end of the 19th, beginning of the 20th century. Wood, bone, feathers, length: 82.5 cm.

123 Eskimo (Uit) man's belt. Sealskin and –fur, walrus ivory.

124 Man's working clothes. Eskimo
(Uit), Alaska, beginning of the 20th
century. Intestinal membranes of sea
creatures, sealskin, beaks and feathers of
birds. Length of the kamleyka: 105 cm,
length of the footwear: 31 cm, height
of the boots: 44 cm.

125 Curing a sealskin. Chukchi, Uelen
village, Chukchi Peninsula, 1970.

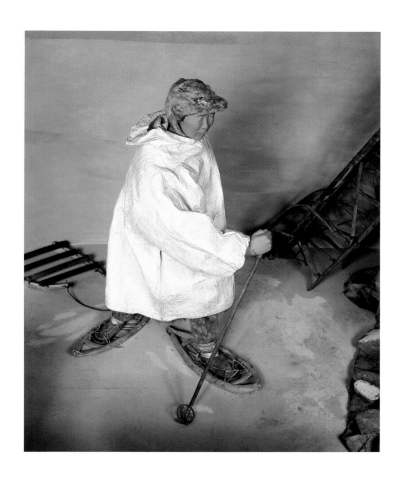

126 Sea hunter.

127 Carved walrus tusk, in colour (primary face). Chukchi, Chukchi Peninsula, 1930s. Length: 57 cm, width: 6 cm.

128 Bucket-handle. Aleut, Aleutian Islands, beginning of the 20th century. Walrus ivory, length: 27 cm.

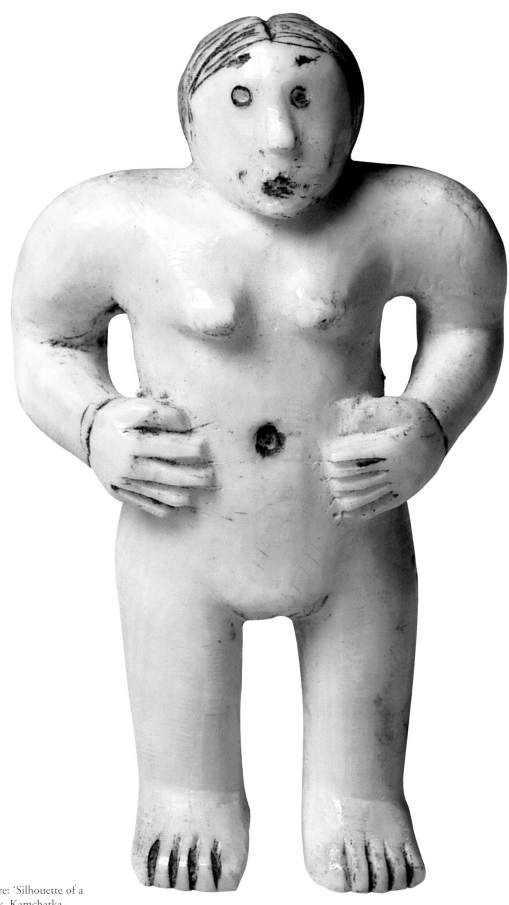

129 Carved miniature: 'Silhouette of a
nude woman'. Koryak, Kamchatka,
1911. Walrus ivory, height: 5.3 cm.

130 Carved miniature: 'Before the
sharing out of the walrus meat'.
Koryak, 1906. Walrus ivory, diameter:
5.8 cm, height: 3.8 cm.

131 *Yukola*, in the process of drying. Kamchatka.

HUNTING AND FISHING

If hunting and fishing are only sidelines for most Siberians, they nonetheless constitute the very foundation of certain cultures, reflecting their original lifestyles. Cultures of this kind include those of the Kets, the Selkup, the Mansis and the Yukaghirs in the taiga, the Shorians, many groups of Evenki and of the Khanty, and the peoples of the Amur River: the Nanai people, the Olchi, the Negidal people, the Oroki, the Orochon people and the Udekhe.

The fishing cultures of the Amur

A natural frontier between Russia and China, the Amur River contains more than a hundred species of fish. Fishing has always therefore been of extreme importance to the local populations. Catching salmon in summer and autumn, and different types of sturgeon and carp in winter, effectively enables the aboriginal communities of the area to live in relative security. It is hunting that in winter is rather the sideline.

When the salmon begin to swim back from the open sea up the Amur River, climbing ever upstream in their urgency to spawn, the local people organize huge fishing parties in the course of which techniques tried and tested over the years bring in truly vast catches. By raising the level of the riverbed with large stones and constructing a large barrier of stones on the upstream side, the men prevent the incoming shoal of salmon from continuing on their course. All at once the stones on the riverbed are removed and the riverbed returns to its normal height, leaving the fish trapped in a much lower pool behind a much taller barrier.

An element central to traditional cultures of the Amur, fish fulfil a multitude of uses in local daily life.

Primarily, of course, they constitute the basic staple diet of the area. They are eaten raw, frozen, smoked, boiled, fried and, particularly, dried. Stocks of salmon and carp, from which *yukola* is prepared, visibly demonstrate the wellbeing of the residents of the Amur's banks, for in summertime, when *yukola* is prepared for the winter, the villages are transformed – from just about anywhere that projects over an empty space hang fish topped and tailed and sliced lengthways into two flat pieces. The Olchi people have no fewer than eight different words and expressions in their language for *yukola*. What is left over from preparing the fish is given to the sledge dogs to eat.

In addition to fish, the people of the Amur like to eat the meat of the elk (moose), bear, reindeer . . . and dog. One of the Nanai people's favourite dishes is *magdan*, which is based on dried caviar crushed and mixed with water or birch sap. In the north, the Yukaghirs of the taiga delight in a rather similar speciality, the *kul'ibakha* – a combination of whortleberries (a type of bilberry), fresh caviar and fish-oil.

The women have a unique process for making something special of the skins of pike, salmon and carp. For several days the skins are left to dry in a particularly shady place. Then they are put on wooden trays and beaten out flat with a mallet. Next, they are rolled around a stick of absinthe, moistened a little, and left for several hours. They are then carefully unrolled, and stretched to their maximum length. Finally, the skins are hung above the hearth and smoked there for two weeks, being taken down before they begin to turn yellow.

132 Hunter with spear in front of his *choom*. Evenki.

133 Eveni adornment to be worn at a
woman's breast. Yakutia, Kolyma
region, 1907. Cured hide (leather),
glass beads, metal, linen, reindeer hair.
Length:112 cm, width: 64 cm.

But fish-skins are used for many purposes other than as food. They are, for instance, much utilized in making summer clothes and footwear. The Nanai people and the Olchi wear vests and shirts made of fish-skin, decorated with embroidery and ordinarily having a round, Chinese-style collar that does up on the right-hand side. In winter, the traditional headgear of the Nanai people is conical in shape with a fur border; it is worn with round fish-skin earmuffs that are furry on the inside and embroidered on the outside. In winter, the fish-skin clothes are lined with cotton. That is the time too for cloaks made of dog-fur or, more often, of reindeer-skin. Shoes, and even boots, made of fish-skin are light, waterproof and (surprisingly) heat-insulated: during the wintertime they can be padded with dry grasses that keep the feet beautifully warm. This is the customary practice of the peoples not only of the Amur but also of Manchuria and northern China.

Fish-skin also goes into making sails for the birch-bark fishing boats, and can be used in windproof drapes for the windows of wooden houses. In summertime the fishermen go off to live in such cabins in the wetlands. If instead they go hunting or fishing at a distance inland, they take their conical wigwams with them and put them up as and when needed.

Water pollution and other serious problems caused by Soviet domination have badly disrupted the ethnic cultures that depend on fishing. All too many of their traditional and ancestral ways of going about things have now been lost forever.

Hunting in the taiga

For thousands of years the elk and the (wild) reindeer have been the primary game animals in Siberia. The people who live by hunting ungulates lead a nomadic life based upon the seasonal migrations of these animals in spring and in autumn. In winter, the inhabitants of the taiga tend instead to hunt fur-bearing prey, such as squirrel or the marten-like sable. Most Evenki legends revolve around hunting, either alone or as a group, for reindeer, for elk, and for birds – and they make no mention whatever of tracking down fur-bearing animals, an activity that spread into the area only after the arrival of the Russians and the imposition of the yassak (the requirement of tribute paid in furs).

Elk and reindeer hunting provides the Evenki and the Eveni with all the essentials for eating, housing, clothing, and making objects for everyday use. The most intensive hunting takes place at the beginning of spring. Wearing skis, the hunters chase the quarry down, on and on until it is exhausted. Of course there are other techniques. Some use the lure – perhaps a male reindeer cunningly arranged with its antlers entwined within a leather thong. In a confrontation with another male, a male generally locks horns – and doing so now will entrap those antlers in the leather thong too. The hunters, who have been following their live lure by keeping it on a very long leash, take immediate advantage of the entanglement by killing the wild reindeer. In the region around the Amur and Lake Baikal, the Evenki have another method: they use a decoy made of birch-bark (*orevun*) to imitate the rutting-call of the male reindeer. Other (real) reindeer race to remonstrate with this upstart trespasser on their territory . . . and pay the price. Formerly armed with long spears and metal bows, the aboriginal hunters have, since the advent of the Russians, adopted the rifle.

113

Most of the peoples of the taiga hunt fur-bearing animals for the money in it. From autumn on, they take to areas where there are plenty of squirrels and sables, and spread themselves out all over the taiga. Those hunters who possess reindeer travel as nomads with the whole of their families. Those hunters who don't instead group up in twos and threes for the duration of the winter, leaving their wives back at the encampment. They go on skis as long as a man's height and as broad as two thumbs – skis in Siberia are usually made of thin conifer wood, although when the snow is particularly deep a layer of reindeer-skin may be added underneath (as with boots, the reindeer skin is from the lower part of the legs of the animals). With the aid of a stick the hunters supervise matters from a sledge mounted on ski-runners.

Apart from ungulates (elk and reindeer) and fur-bearing animals, which are hunted all over Siberia, there are some creatures that are not hunted because – at least among certain ethnic groups – they have totemic associations with the people. Such creatures include the eagle, the swan, the owl, the stork, the bear, the wolf and the tiger.

Rarely undertaken, the hunting of the bear is in any case strictly regulated, for this animal – so sympathetic in appearance, and so human in intelligence – inspires both fear and respect among the ethnic communities of Siberia. So much so that for many it is taboo to use the ordinary word for 'bear' and kennings (pseudonymous phrases) are used instead: 'the old man of the forest', 'the grandfather', 'the master of the taiga' and so forth. Indeed, the bear is the focus of a highly developed cult among certain peoples, notably the Nivkhi, the Negidal people and the Khanty.

The wolf, because it hunts down the same quarry as men, is considered by them to be their equal, and in consequence is seldom hunted itself. The Evenki of the east call the animal 'son', 'greyhair' or 'naughty boy', and believe that it is a heinous crime to cause the death of wolfcubs. In winter, however, the Chukchis hunt the wolf with the aid of a redoubtable weapon. A piece of bony cartilage from a whale's head is carved into an extremely spiky shape, rolled up small and tied in that position with string. It is then steeped in water until it ices up. The string that kept it together is drawn off, and the resultant iced ball is smeared with animal fat. It is then placed in the path of the wolf which, when it finds it, swallows it. The ice melts quickly in the internal warmth of the stomach, the sharp spikes emerge and unbend to pierce the stomach wall of the wolf, and so cause its death.

By tradition it is the men, in Siberia, who devote themselves to hunting and fishing, while the women are charged with domestic duties – keeping the fire going, putting up and taking down the *choom*, tanning the hides, stitching together the clothes, looking after the children . . . Yet among many of the peoples it is by no means unusual for women to go hunting, alone or together with the men – and to be as successful at it. That is certainly the case among, for example, the Yukaghirs. Some of their old women are renowned for their hunting prowess, and include even bears among their hunting trophies.

134 Yukaghir in traditional hunting costume – skis with reindeer-skin bases – in front of a *urasa*.

135 Haymaking in central Yakutia.

136 An old Yukaghir story-teller —
despite being a woman, renowned for
her hunting prowess and her artistic
skills.

137 Horse dressed up for a festival.
Yakutia.

THE TURKIC AND MONGOLIAN ANIMAL-BREEDERS

In the steppes of southern Siberia, the Khakass people, the Altai people, the Tuva people, the Buryats and, further north and just into the tundra, the Yakuts have for centuries based their culture on raising horses and breeding horned animals. These Turkic and Mongolian peoples also farm sheep on the southern plains, while in the mountainous regions they additionally herd reindeer – strictly for transportation purposes. Further north still, in Arctic zones, the Yakuts have copied reindeer-herding methods from the Evenki.

Nomadic in former times, these communities have during the course of the 20th century become partly – well, totally – residential in habit. To be sure, a few groups lead a sort of semi-nomadic way of life with their animals, divided between winter pasturages and summer pasturages.

The traditional mode of dwelling for all these peoples is the Mongolian-style yurt. Mobile when made mainly of cloth, pretty solidly static when built of wooden logs, the yurt varies from region to region not only in construction materials but also in shape – round, square, octagonal, and more besides. The roof of the yurt is held up in the centre by a wide post at an angle, which also acts as a chimney-flue. The entrance to the yurt, among the Buryats, is oriented towards the south; among the Yakuts it is towards the east. In some areas in summer, the yurt is replaced by a wigwam-like conical tent.

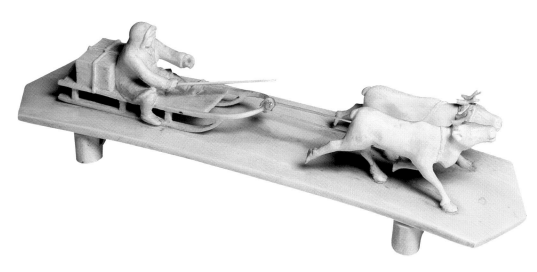

138 Sculpture: 'Reindeer-owner and sledge'. Yakut, 1955. Mammoth ivory, length: 17 cm, width: 4.5 cm, height: 5.5 cm.

139 Koryak nomads' yurt. Okhotsk
region, 1896–1897.

140 Evenki on reindeer-back. Yenisey
Province, beginning of the
20th century.

Summertime, among these groups, is dedicated to agricultural activities, and there is much to do, especially the hay-making which ensures reserve supplies of food for much of the livestock. In the winter the cattle and horses, left to their own devices in grasslands, have to find food for themselves under the snow.

Breeding cattle and horses for adaptation to the conditions of Siberia has been the work of the Yakuts. Indeed, the physical particulars of a Yakut horse bear witness to its adaptation to the rigours of the climate in the Siberian north – compact and small in stature, with a long shaggy coat, the animal can withstand extremely low temperatures (below –50°C/–58°F) and is quite capable of turning up its food independently by stamping on the frozen ground with its hoofs. It is the horse that is the focus of the Yakut cultural heritage. According to one legend it was the first creature on the earth, the ancestor of humankind. And certainly in former times the horse provided the Yakuts with all the resources needed for their lifestyle – meat, leather, hide, transportation, everything. Cattle, introduced by these same Yakuts into the northern regions of Siberia rather later, have since taken over as the central pillar of their way of life. Nonetheless, the breed of cattle developed by them over the centuries is today on the edge of extinction. They possess the very same qualities as the Yakut horse – small, hardy, with a shag-

141 Small Yakut rug. Horsehair and cotton.

gy hide and a reproduction rate that is relatively slow – although their milk is particularly rich, in terms of nutritive value, in comparison with that of ordinary cows. But it was because of the sluggishness in the overall rate of reproduction that the Soviet authorities decided that other types of cattle must be brought in . . . and following the resultant multiple cross-breeding that then ensued, the Yakut cattle have today all but vanished completely.

The semi-nomadic way of life of the Turkic and Mongolian peoples of Siberia is closely linked with the herds of horses they move with twice every year – in spring and in autumn – to new areas of pasturage.

In Yakutia, horses live in a semi-wild state. On festive occasions the Yakuts pay special attention to the tack – by tradition, the standard equestrian accoutrements comprise a saddle ornamented with plaques of embossed silver, a pair of stirrups, a bridle and a smallish saddle-blanket also decorated with bright bits and pieces. In the summertime, both horses and cattle wander freely over the great plains that characterize the traditional countryside of the Yakuts – the alas, a vast heathland bestrewn with scattered lakes surrounded by forests. In the evenings, the cattle return to the byre for milking, either following a leader or driven there by boys on horseback.

142 Toys shaped like horses. Yakut, Yakutia, 1908, 1910. Wood, length i) 30 cm, ii) 23 cm, height: i) 15 cm, ii) 22 cm.

143 Yakuts in traditional costume, with a scythe. Beginning of the 20th century.

144 Wedding saddle for a woman. Yakut, 1959, 1909, 1925-1926. Wood, metal, deerskin, horsehair, linen, other fabrics, horse-hide, pearls, glass beads. Saddle: length: 55 cm, width: 27cm, height: 34 cm. Stirrups: length: 19 cm, width: 14 cm. *****: length: 156 cm, width: 89 cm. Saddle-cover: length: 93 cm, width: 69 cm.

145 Nuptial bag. Yakut, 1909. Reindeer-hide, pearls, glass beads, cured reindeer-skin. Length: 79 cm, width: 55–62 cm.

Left to roam the pastures in summer, the cattle in winter are fed on hay in *khoton* – sheds specifically adapted for extreme temperatures. In past centuries the *khoton* were pretty well no more than extensions of the yurt, and indeed still retain similarities. Like the Yakut style of yurt (*balaghan*), the *khoton* is made of wood, has sloping sides and a flat roof covered with earth. Its walls are shored up from the outside with clay and cow-dung. It is a system that ensures the cows are warm in winter – and in summer the blocks of dried cow-dung are removed and burned to keep the multitudinous mosquitoes at bay.

In central Yakutia, despite the Sovietization, the Yakut villages preserve their local colour thanks both to the *khoton* and to the *ambar* (cereal granaries), rectangular buildings of wood with flat roofs covered in earth and, in summertime, with vegetation. Winter yurts and the summertime tents (*urasa*) have, on the other hand, now completely disappeared in favour of Russian-style wooden houses. Yurts nonetheless remain in use in some southern regions of Siberia.

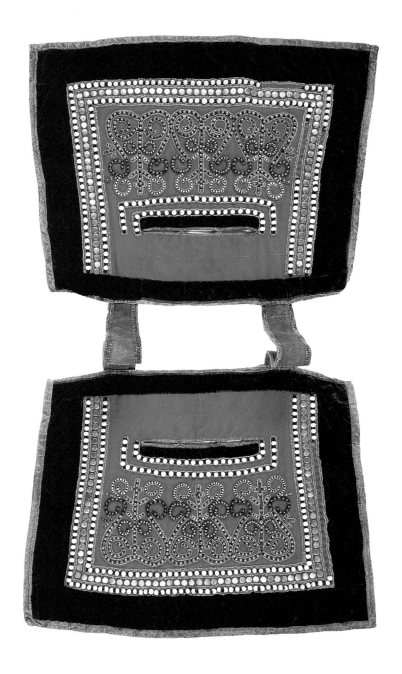

146 Yakut saddle-bag. Yakutsk, 1904.
Linen, cured hide (leather), glass beads,
pearls, metal. Length: 62 cm, width:
51 cm.

147 Woman preparing food near a stove inside a yurt. 1913.

148 Kamtchak, 1897-1897

149 Urban Yakut on horseback.
Yakutia, 1906.

The food-products of cattle-raising – meat and milk – constitute the primary diet of the Turkic and Mongolian peoples. Specialities involving meat and milk dominate their eating habits, topped up with fish, which in turn form an appreciable proportion of the diet of those who live on the shores of Lake Baikal and on the banks of the Lena. Additional delicacies are those brought home after hunting and, in summer, after scavenging for berries and fungi. A drink consumed amid some ritual by the Yakuts is the famous *koumiss*, fermented mare's milk, quaffed in large quantities at the height of the festival of *Isyakh* in June from huge bowls carved in wood – the *ayakh* or *choron*. Quite different is the daily dish of the Yakuts out in the fields: *kuortchekh* – whipped cream embellished with whortleberries. The preferred meat dishes of these northerly people are frozen raw foal meat and *stroganina* (frozen raw fish). Bowls, dishes and much of the household utensils are made mostly of wood or of birch bark.

As elsewhere in Siberia, traditional costume is no longer worn at any time other than on ceremonial occasions. Among the Yakuts it is the women who are then more colourfully dressed, for onto their costumes are sewn the furs of marmot, beaver and sable. The lining is of red and green cloth or even Chinese silk. The outside is decorated with embroidery, beads and silver ornaments. This form of costume, which in the old days was passed down from mother to daughter, is completed by a fur hat crowned with a little cloth top-piece with pointed edges. On the hat are many silver decorations, while similar carved silver ornaments of more complex design hang from the wearer's ears and as wider panels over the breast and back.

Metalworking, and specifically silversmithing, is a craft that has been much practised over the centuries and that flourishes even now in Yakutia. Women there continue to wear their traditional jewellery – especially rings, necklaces and decorated earrings. In addition, the Yakuts carve and make sculptures out of wood and, from the 18th century, out of mammoth-tusk ivory – earrings, bracelets, ornamental combs and trinket-boxes, little statuettes, and so on. Such handicrafts merely add lustre to the skills they demonstrate in working with skins and furs.

*

But besides these strictly practical considerations, the lifestyles that represent the cultural heritage of the peoples of the north revolve around many traditions, rituals, customs, rules and taboos that flow from a specific way of thinking, a highly particular conception of the world . . .

150 *Serghe* – a ceremonial post to tie up horses to.

151 Heap of manure (right) and a pile of human excrement put out into the streets of a village.

152 *Ambar* (cereal granaries).

153 *Choron* – containers for *koumiss*.
Yakut, 1903, end of the 19th, beginning of the 20th century. Wood, height
i) 21 cm, ii) 56 cm, diameter: i) 13 cm,
ii) 21 cm.

154 Strainer for making *koumiss*.
Yakut, beginning of the 20th century.
Wood, length: 103 cm, diameter of
collecting jar: 18 cm.

155 Yakuts sitting down to lunch.
1911.

156 Yurt (traditional Yakut winter residence).

157 Summer tent.

158 Container for koumiss used in the Isyakh celebrations. Yakut, 1906. Wood, metal, height: 22 cm, diameter: 32–33 cm.

159 Plate for serving guests. Yakut, 1909. Wood, metal, height: 23.5 cm, diameter: 65 cm.

160 Box in which to keep objects of traditional culture. Yakut, 1908. Birch bark, glass beads, horsehair, wood, skin. Height: 14 cm, diameter: 14–17 cm.

161 Yakuts in national costume making *koumiss* for the festival of Isyakh, 1910.

162 The festival of Isyakh. Part of the exhibition 'Siberian Peoples: End of the Nineteenth Century to the Beginning of the Twentieth Century'. Yakutia.

163 Boxes. Yakut, beginning of the 20th century. Wood, i) length: 31 cm, width: 11 cm, height: 7.5 cm, ii) height: 17 cm, diameter: 5 cm.

164 Box in which to keep valuable furs or money. Yakut, 1906. Birch bark, mica, paper, horsehair, hide. Height: 37 cm, diameter at base: 57 cm, diameter at opening: 48 cm.

165 M. N. Lavramova, actress, during the Akha Theatre festival, Yakutsk

166 A Yakut bracelet.

167 Mosquito fan. Yakut, 1908. Wolverine fur, wood, metal, pearls, hide. Length: 50 cm, length of handle: 13 cm.

168 Yakuts in traditional festive costume. Yakutia, 1906.

169 Man's belt. Yakut, 1971. Metal, hide, length: 126 cm, width: 7 cm.

170 Fragment of a man's belt. Yakut, 1971. Metal, hide.

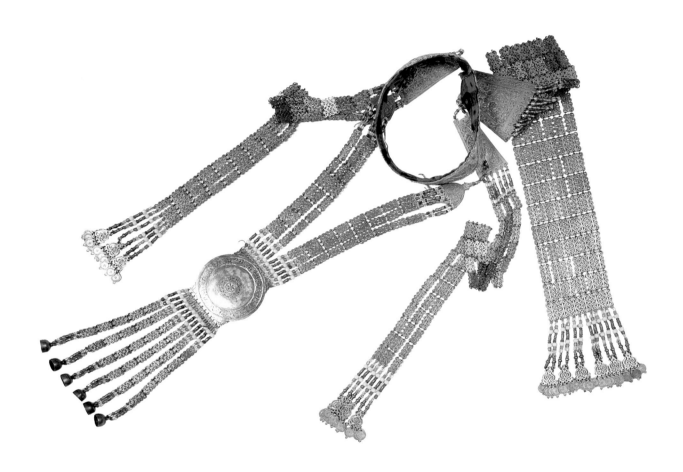

171 Woman's earrings, man's ring.
Yakut, Yakutsk, 1959. Metal, length of
earrings: 8.7 cm, diameter of ring:
2.2 cm.

172 Head decoration. Yakut, 1903.
Silver, cloth, pearls. Length: 97 cm.

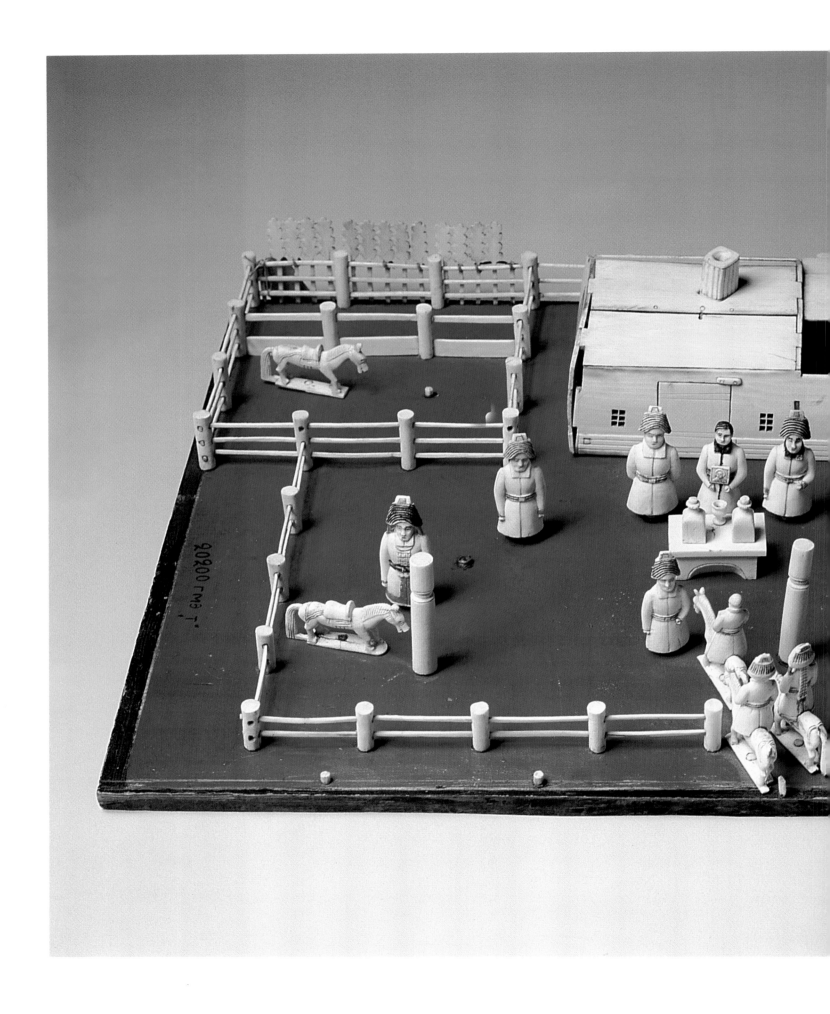

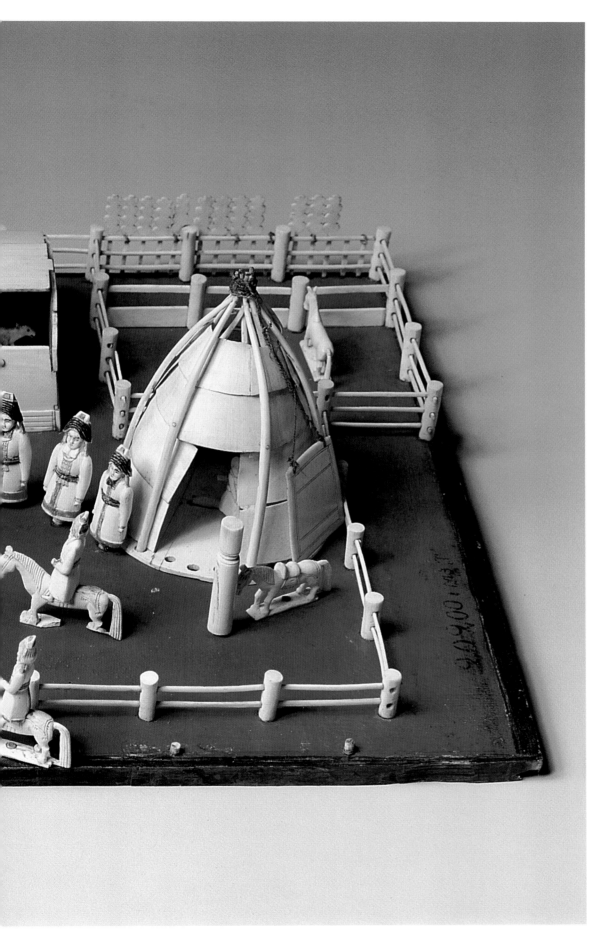

173 Model of a Yakut court. Yakut, beginning of the 20th century. Mammoth ivory, wood, length: 54 cm, width: 36 cm.

TRADITIONAL WAYS OF LIFE, AND SHAMANISM

WORLD-CONCEPTS AND MYTHOLOGIES

For thousands of years the peoples of Siberia have evolved and preserved their own original and diverse cultures, naturally including a highly developed spiritual element, founded on the common basis of a holistic approach that incorporates animism, spiritism and shamanism. Concepts of the world, and of humankind's place in it, corresponding to the insights of these societies have encouraged complete systems of religious beliefs, myths, rituals and festivals, many as inspiring in a poetic sense as they are symbolically.

The aboriginal peoples of Siberia tend towards a dualist philosophy, or at least a belief in two major planes of existence: the human and the universal. Everything, natural or synthetic is regarded as existing as a whole that nonetheless comprises two distinct parts, one visible (the material and palpable) and the other invisible (the immaterial, on the abstract plane). The human body, like the bodies of all the animals, is no more than a covering of flesh that houses an 'energy' – a life force that anthropologists, depending on which ethnic group they are talking about, interpret as a 'spirit-soul', a 'breath of life' or indeed a 'vital spark'. The universal plane, to the peoples of Siberia, comprises a number of superimposed layers (the number differs between mythological systems), but it too is primarily in two parts, just like the visible world of humans, animals and plants. The residents of this invisible world are the spirits and the gods.

174 Shaman with representations of the spirits. Evenki, Yenisey Province, beginning of the 20th century.

175 Ceremony at sunrise at the
beginning of the traditional Yakut
festival of Isahar.

Spirit-souls

To the aboriginal peoples of Siberia, a person possesses certainly one 'spirit-soul', sometimes several. Certain beliefs linked to the notion of the human spirit-soul occur within most Siberian cultures. For example, the spirit-soul has the power to free itself from the human body and travel independently – this is what dreams are. But the spirit-soul can also be forcibly possessed by universal spirits; it is this that causes disease and, in the most extreme case, death, followed by a return to the natural sphere from which it first came and where it becomes once more available to future human lives.

The Nenets believe that every person has a 'spirit-soul breath' indivisibly accom-panied during life by a 'shade' (*sidiang*) which survives death. The Nanai people picture the spirit-souls of children (*omiya*) in the form of little birds come down from the skies to dwell for a time in the wombs of their mothers to be. This spirit-soul then gradually metamorphoses as the child grows, matures and ages, until at last it finally departs from its fleshly cover-ing on the seventh day after death, thereafter taking three years to sink down into the Lower World.

According to the traditional notions of the Yakuts, each person possesses three spirit-souls: one is the spirit-soul of earth (*buor-kout*), another is the spirit-soul of air (*salgyn-kout*) and the last is the spirit-soul mother (*iye-kout*). The spirit-soul of earth is responsible for the health and the physical wholeness of the person; the spirit-soul of air monitors how the person gets on in life, dealing with the environment and with other people; and the spirit-soul mother is in charge of the person's consciousness and capacity for reasoned thought. These three spirit-souls together form an entity consid-ered to represent the life force (*kout-sur*); on its integral harmony rests the continued wellbeing of the person.

176 Ritual offering to the spirits of fire. Eveni.

177 'Steel', with the family protector-deities. Chukchi Peninsula, 1896. Height: 58 cm, width: 11 cm.

THE THREE WORLDS

In their mythologies, the aboriginal peoples of Siberia ordinarily represent the universe as made up of three worlds: the Upper World (or World of the Heavens), the Lower World (or Underworld) and, between them, the Middle World (the Earth) – the domain of living things.

The Upper World

The World of the Heavens is where the superior universal spirits live, spirit-masters of the natural elements (the taiga, the waters, horned animals, reindeer and so on) and of the cosmic elements (the sun, the moon, the stars, the winds and so on). Such spirits are powerful deities present at, if not contributory to, the Creation of the world, and who appear in the myths and legends of these northern peoples in anthropomorphic guise. These myths and legends present a veritable host of accounts of the Creation.

Creation myths

One day, a girl fleeing from the Upper World fell into the sea together with her only possession, a reindeer. To save the life of the mistress on his back, the reindeer implored the girl to sacrifice him. The girl did so, and killed the reindeer – who at once changed his form. His skin turned into the dry land; the furry part of his hide turned into the forests; his skull and his bones turned into the mountains and the valleys; his dying sigh gave birth to the winds.
(Eveni myth)

178 Representation of the protector-deity of the family. Koryak, Kamchatka, 1904–1907. Stone, reindeer-hide, wolverine fur, glass beads, pearls cloth. Height: 22 cm.

In the beginning, all there was water. Then there were also two brother Creator-gods. The elder brother, the embodiment of Evil, resided in the Upper World, whereas his younger sibling, the embodiment of Good, lived in the Lower World. One day, Grebe – assistant to the younger god – stirred up a little bit of dry land on the bottom of the ocean, took it upon himself to bring it up to the surface of the water, and looked after it there. The two brothers each found themselves wondering what they, in their own ways, could do for the new site. The elder created, among other things, all the animals of which the flesh is inedible by humans. The younger meanwhile chose to give life to those animals that can be eaten. It was in this way that the younger of the two brothers, with the help of Grebe, became ruler of the Upper World too.
(Evenki myth)

It is said that at that time only a single conscious being lived on the Earth – Apapel', the Great Raven, the beneficent and eternal Creator. The Earth was exactly the same then as it is today, with the same plants and the same animals . . . But there were no people. So Apapel' decided to create several thousand of them. After a hundred years' work the beings modelled in clay by Apapel' formed so high a mountain that the Creator found himself able to step straight into heaven. Having raised himself to that great height, he blew upon the mountain of clay beings beneath him, sending them scattering and tumbling all over the place, and he bestowed a spirit-soul on each. Those who fell all the way to the ground-soil became men; those who found themselves caught up on the branches of trees became women.
(Chukchi myth)

179 The delta of the Lena.

157

180 Amulet. Aleut, Aleutian Islands,
end of the 19th, beginning of the 20th
century. Bone, glass beads, hide and
intestinal membranes of sea creatures,
tendons. Height: 12 cm.

181 Amulet. Aleut, Aleutian Islands,
end of the 19th, beginning of the 20th
century. Bone, pearls, tendons. Height:
7.4 cm.

182 Bow related to the solar cult
among the Yukaghirs of the taiga
(Nelemnoe).

183 Tree sacred to a family.

The raven, though not as Creator himself but as an assistant to the Creator in the work of Creation, is also to be found in the mythologies of the Koryaks, the Itelmen people, the Chukchis and the Aleuts. According to the Chukchi myths it was the raven that fashioned the relief-map of the world, carving out with his beak the boundaries of the lakes and the courses of the rivers. It was he who created the birds, the fish, the sea creatures, the bear, the wolf and the fox. In the myths of the Itelmen people, Kouth the raven plays an identical role. The valleys and the mountains represent the tracks imprinted in the ground by his reindeer sledge. The rainbows sometimes to be seen in the sky are the reflection of the colours embroidered on his fiery cloak.

Among the Yakuts, the Creator is given the name Urung Aiyi Toyon. It is he who created the earth, the air, humankind and the animals, and who gave them the capacity for fertilization, the power of reproduction. According to one of the myths, the Earth as created initially by Urung Aiyi Toyon was extremely beautiful and extremely smooth. It was only after it had for a very long time been trampled all over, stamped on, perforated with holes, compacted and damaged by demons (*abaasy*) that it came to have its mountains, its valleys, its plains, lakes and rivers and so forth.

184 Carved miniature: 'Shaman with his spirit-protector, the eagle', 'Shaman with his spirit-protector, an animal'. Koryak, i) Primor'ye, ii) Kamchatka, 1903. Walrus ivory, height: i) 6.8 cm, ii) 7.8 cm, height of the stand: i) 4.5 cm, ii) 3.8 cm.

185 Amulet. Evenki, Yenisey Province, 1910. Wood, cotton cloth, glass beads, metal. Height: 17 cm.

186 *Ojbon*: detail from a Yakut shaman's costume. The *ojbon* is literally a hole that can be penetrated, and ordinarily refers to a hole in the ice for fishing through. In this case, however, it means the 'passage' the shaman must make use of in order to travel to other planes.

163

187 Ancient tomb of a shaman. Yakut,
Yakutia, beginning of the 20th century.

188 Female shaman with drum
surrounded by villagers. Koryak.

189 Shamanic costume. Evenki,
extreme eastern Siberia, end of the 19th
century. Deerskin, fur, cotton velvet,
plastic buttons, metal, sealskin, cloth,
pearls, glass beads, felt. Tunic length:
104 cm, from the collar: 57 cm, width
of collar: 36 cm. Headpiece – height:
20 cm, diameter: 21 cm.

190 Shamanic costume. Evenki, extreme eastern Siberia, end of the 19th century. Deerskin, fur, cotton velvet, plastic buttons, metal, sealskin, cloth, pearls, glass beads, felt. Tunic length: 104 cm, from the collar: 57 cm, width of collar: 36 cm. Headpiece – height: 20 cm, diameter: 21 cm.

191 Shamanic costume. Evenki, Lower
Tunguska Basin, beginning of the 20th
century. Cured hide (leather), glass
beads, metal, bearskin, cotton cloth.
Tunic length: 96 cm, from the
decoration on the chest: 73 cm,
width: 17 cm.

192 Shamanic costume. Yakut,
end of the 19th, beginning of the
20th century. Cured hide, metal,
length: 82 cm.

193 Details from a shamanic costume.

The Lower World

Situated beneath the ground, the Lower World is the kingdom of the dead, the realm of shades, the haunt of all kinds of evil-minded spirits, demons and mythical monsters. The peoples of Siberia tend to think of the way of life for the dead in the Lower World as being much the same as – or at any rate not too far different from – the way people live on the surface of the Earth. The Evenki, for example, in their traditions see life in the Lower World as following the same cycles and the same sort of arrangements as they see in their own – belonging to clans that in turn belong to larger tribes, living in *chooms*, wearing the same kind of clothes, hunting and fishing. Indeed, the dead are only different from living humans in that they eat nothing but locusts, have no body temperature and do not breathe or have a heartbeat. The Eveni people, on the other hand, reckon the Lower World to be the diametric opposite of the Middle World. Summertime on the Earth's surface corresponds to winter in the realm of the dead; daytime is night-time; and so forth. The Yakuts conceive of the dead as having eyes of clear ice but leading lives otherwise identical to their own – except with a half-sun by day to complement the half-moon by night.

194 A shaman's footwear. Evenki. Salmon-skin.

195 Shaman's drum. Evenki, Lower Tunguska Basin, beginning of the 20th century. Hide, wood, metal, pearls. Height: 95 cm, width: 50 cm.

196 The ritual relating to the spirit of
fire. Yakutia.

197 The sacred tree of a shaman.

198 Part of a shaman's *choom*. Evenki,
Yenisey Province, beginning of the
20th century.

199 Koryak woman in the process of
making welcome the spirit-masters of
the semi-domesticated reindeer at the
traditional autumn festival of Koryak
reindeer-herders.

The Middle World

The Middle World is the domain of living things – humankind, animals and plants. However, people are never genuinely alone. They are constantly surrounded by spirits of all types, good and evil. In fact, the aboriginal peoples of Siberia live in perpetual fear of these spirits, convinced that diseases, famines, epidemics and other misfortunes are all the result of the spirits' wish for vengeance or general malevolence. And they take great care, accordingly, not to give them cause for offence, not to provoke their anger by inappropriate behaviour. To protect themselves against the baleful influences of the spirits, the ethnic groups in Siberia have recourse to all sorts of 'magical' procedures and animist rites – spells, prayers, ritual practices, sacred amulets, symbols and images worn on clothing or tattooed on the body.

Traditionally, the Chukchis, the Koryaks and the Uit (Eskimos) protect themselves from evil spirits by wearing amulets that they never take off. The more individuals feel themselves vulnerable, the more they endeavour to protect themselves as best they can. Some believe that the spirit-soul has the power, if in real danger, to take refuge inside a single glass bead. Pregnant women, young mothers and infants at the breast are all protected with appropriately targeted adornments by way of earrings, bracelets, rings, bead necklets and so forth. The current means of ensuring the protection of a child is to fix either to the collar of the child's vest or to a wristband a tiny humanoid figurine made of willow bark. This is the type of talisman worn by reindeer-herders on their belts when they leave the family encampment knowing that they will be away for a protracted period.

Finally, another kind of amulet altogether comprises pebbles, particularly pebbles that have a strange shape, collected from the tundra or from a coastline or riverbank.

200 Pipe to smoke tobacco at public reunions. Chukchi, the Anadyr area, Primor'ye, end of the 19th, beginning of the 20th century. Wood, reindeer antler, cured hide (leather), sealskin, reindeer-hide, metal. Length: 87.5 cm.

201 Drumstick for a shamanic drum. Evenki. Wood, bearskin, metal.

202 Request for future abundance during a ritual for Chukchi reindeer-herders.

203 Head ornament for the seriously ill. Eveni, the Anadyr area, 1910. Cured hide (leather), reindeer-hide, sealskin. Width: 31 cm, length of pendants: 35 cm, overall height: 61 cm.

204 Tinder-box. Eveni, coastline of the Sea of Okhotsk, 1920s. Hide, pearls, glass beads, cloth, metal. Height: 12 cm.

The spirit-masters

In the traditional concepts of the aboriginal peoples of Siberia, all the different things that together make up the surface world – the animal species, the types of terrain and landmarks (mountains, the taiga, the tundra, lakes, rivers and so on), and the natural and cosmic elements (fire, water, wind, sun…) – are under the control of the spirit-masters, themselves the object of great veneration by the people. These are spirits that are again conceived in anthropomorphic terms. So, for example, the spirit-master of fire is sometimes represented as a little old man, emaciatedly thin, dressed in clothing that is richly embroidered. Sitting on the back of a leader of the herd, he has the power to guide wild reindeer to where the hunters are waiting. He is present at the slaughter of any reindeer to make sure that humans pay due respect in their ritual observances. If the humans fail in this duty, he may decide to punish them by causing the reindeer to flee far from the course of any future hunt. Among the Yakuts, a successful return from hunting is attributed to the goodwill of the spirit-master of the forests, an old man of enormous height and particularly cheerful demeanour who is known as Baai-Bainai.

The traditional way of life for the aboriginal peoples of Siberia is thus set about with extremely strict rules of conduct to be adhered to in respect of different spirits. Bans and taboos must be rigorously observed and all the various rituals, customs and festivities must be scrupulously performed at due times, if harmonious coexistence between humans and spirits is to be maintained. Only if such conditions are fully complied with can collective and personal wellbeing be assured.

Communication between Worlds

There are ways of passing between the three Worlds, but what those ways are like varies from one mythological system to another.

According to Evenki stories, the three Worlds are linked at the source of the mystical (and mythical) river Enghedik, which has many tributaries that flow in the four great directions: south, east, south-east and north-east. Each tributary is allocated to one Evenki clan. In order to reach the Upper World – something that the shaman alone has the power to do – it is necessary to follow this river to its source, to climb on ever upstream, until you get to the World Tree which affords access to the other Worlds, both Upper and Lower.

The notion of a World Tree is also found in other mythological systems. The Yakuts, for instance, venerate sacred trees they call *Aal Kuduk Mas*, which they regard as thinking and moral beings continually preoccupied with the wellbeing of the inhabitants of the Middle World. These trees are in contact through their roots with the Lower World and, through their highest branches, with the nine heavenly lands that comprise the Upper World. Tradition demands that every clan, every Yakut family, has its own sacred tree which it deeply venerates as the visible link between those now living and their ancestors gone before. Generally, it is a tree that presents certain characteristic features, such as unusual height, a gnarled trunk and a particularly poignant location.

Evenki myths declare that Polaris, the Pole Star, is the point at which the Middle World touches the Upper World, while rock fissures, chasms, caves and other abysses in the ground are all capable of taking one down to the Lower World. The peoples of north-eastern Siberia believe that the doorway between all three Worlds lies at a point directly beneath the Pole Star. And the Pole Star again has a special significance in the cosmogony of the Chukchis, who think of it by tradition as a 'nail' to which are fixed all the other stars of the celestial vault. When the star reaches its highest point in the heavens, a great chasm opens underneath it through which a person may travel from one World to another, for Polaris is visible in every World of the universe.

The origins of the shaman

In the past of long ago, the paths to and from the different levels of the universe might be freely used by ordinary men and women, long and arduous though such journeys were for most of them. But people from the Middle World were not able to communicate with residents of the other Worlds, for these residents had their own unintelligible language, they were unable to see humans and they fell ill at once if somehow they came into contact with them. And so, all at once, humans were put under a restriction to stay on their own Earth. In this way, and for these reasons, travelling from one World to another became at a stroke the prerogative of a new caste of humans – the shamans, who could 'qualify' as intercessors between human people and the spirits. Around such men, the shamans, what is now one of the oldest religions in the world evolved and developed: shamanism.

205 Ritual mask. Koryak, Kamchatka,
1930s. Wood, tendons, length:
30.7 cm, width: 16 cm.

206 Ritual mask. Koryak, Kamchatka,
1911. Cured reindeer-hide, cloth,
walrus tusk. Length: 27 cm, width:
22 cm.

207 Ritual mask. Koryak, Kamchatka,
1930s. Wood, cotton thread,
length: 22.3 cm, width: 11.2 cm.

SHAMANISM AND THE SHAMANS OF SIBERIA

Shamanism is an extremely ancient form of religion, founded on a combination of meta-physical world-concepts and on mythology, taking for granted the existence of a parallel world and a pantheon of deities. On a broader scale it represents the outward expression of a complex metaphysical system superimposed upon the visible 'real' world.

The phenomenon of shamanism nonetheless revolves around the personality of the shaman himself and his activities.

The role of the shaman in society

The word *shaman*, in the original Evenki language, means an individual for whom the role of mediation between humans and spirits is at one and the same time a prerogative and a duty. Only a shaman, following a period of apprenticeship, is capable of travelling across the different levels of the universe and to come into contact with inhabitants of the other Worlds. Each time he does, it is with a clear and precise objective, and at the behest of a group of people or of a single person. Most often, the shaman is asked to resolve a problem, or to relieve an intolerable situation, but the request may alternatively be to ensure a favourable outcome, to predict the future or to influence natural (particu-larly climatic) conditions.

In former times the shaman was himself the object of fear and awe amid the social communities of Siberia. His authority, however, remained proportional to the success of his 'mediations' and he did not otherwise enjoy any special privileges.

Victims of harsh and widespread persecution during the Soviet period, shamans are now comparatively rare. In certain regions, only the tribal elders retain any memory of them at all.

How to become a shaman

To be of one sex or the other makes little difference to a shaman in working life, for shamans frequently take on the characteristics of either sex. Yet the basic rule for a shaman – who might be a woman just as naturally as a man – is to have as a spirit-protector one who is technically of the opposite sex. In the meantime, female shamans may earn as excellent a reputation as any male ones, but they are held to lose their powers during each pregnancy and for some years after giving birth.

There are three ways in which shamans in Siberia receive their gifts. The most common is to be born into them, but it is possible also to become a shaman after a good deal of accredited self-examination or by being chosen to fulfil the position. Among the Nenets, a mark in the shape of an elongated drum somewhere on the body of an infant could well indicate that the child may in due course take up the profession of shaman.

Choosing a neophyte to be a shaman of the future happens most often when the neophyte is at the adolescent stage. A spirit-protector appears in a dream to the chosen one and summarily demands – leaving the young boy or girl absolutely no choice in the matter – that he or she joins the profession. Where a person wishes to become a shaman through self-examination, the applicant spends considerable time and effort in introspective research so that a spirit-protector may make himself or herself known.

Whether destined by heredity, by selection or by introspection, the first stage for a would-be shaman is to go into isolation – in the forest or in a solitary residence – for an indeterminate length of time. During this period he or she must fast, chant invocations and be prepared to submit to any initiatory tests that the spirit-protector might impose upon him or her (including tests of asceticism or celibacy).

Only after this period of isolation has come to an end is it held to be the time for the novice's actual initiation as shaman into the bosom of the community. This takes place under the direction of an experienced shaman (who may be a close relative), and represents the novice's taking upon himself or herself the means of passing between the different Worlds, and the knowledge of the paths by which to travel to meet the spirits, and to establish contact and communicate with them. The initiation ceremony ends with the master-shaman's submitting the pupil to a ritual of dedication to his or her shamanic duties.

The attributes of a shaman

The new shaman then receives the badges of office – the clothing, the drum, the staff, amulets and so forth – a sort of 'trousseau' put together under strictly monitored conditions by the whole community. Among the Evenki, for example, the shaman's costume may be stitched together only by virgin girls, the various ornaments and metallic pendants for the costume have to be forged by male relatives of the shaman, the decoration of the drum is the task of community wives.

The new shaman is not finally consecrated as such until a ritual has been undertaken to 'activate' the various bits of clothing and equipment he or she has just received. In the course of this, he or she – with others – chants aloud all the beliefs and community lore on the subject of the animal and the tree from which the shamanic drum has been made. The significance of this ritual is to make it quite clear that the shaman can exercise his or her powers only when in possession of all these attributes. It is specifically by dressing in the costume and taking hold of the drum and the staff that the shaman receives the powers essential to effective intercession – the powers constituted by his or her spirit-protectors, of which the most important power is that of being able to journey from one World to another.

The costume of the shaman

The shaman's official costume is distinguishable from ordinary clothing by the cut with which it is specially styled and by the ornaments that hang from it and symbolize the links uniting the shaman with his spirit-protectors. Decorations on the costume include astral, animal and humanoid figures, each positioned according to a precise logic to reflect the composition of the universe and the connections between different elements of Creation. If the main spirit-protector of a shaman is, say, a bird, the costume will be decorated with multiple pendants representing the bird, its feathers, wings and talons. In addition to symbols corresponding to spirit-protectors, the shaman's costume generally also incorporates images of the sun, the moon, the World Tree, the higher spirits and sometimes of the shaman himself on his psychic mount.

208 Koryak woman: the roof of a *yarang*. The closing of the traditional autumn festival of the Koryak reindeer-herders.

209 Detail of the inside of a *yarang*. Chukchi, Chukotka, 1970.

These decorative items on the shamanic costume are made out of various materials – metal, bone, fabric, leather, fur – and with them all in place, the costume is not surprisingly quite heavy to wear. For this reason it is customary for a shaman to have assistants (generally close relatives) to help in his activities.

At the same time, the attributes on the shamanic costume vary widely between one region and another, as much in the materials used to make them and the ritual procedures required in doing so as in their quantity and their nomenclature. For example, the shamanic drum is of basic importance to the religious beliefs of the Chukchis – or most of them anyway – surpassing even the significance accorded the costume. Yet to the Evenki, conversely, it is the costume and its ornamentation that is paramount.

The shaman's drum and staff

The drum and the staff are both of considerable importance to the shaman and what he does. As with the costume, these badges of office represent an image of the cosmic world, an outward and visible sign of the connection with spirit-protectors. Among many ethnic groups in Siberia, the staff is illustrated with representations (drawn, painted, carved, etc.) of the spirit-protectors in the form of animals or birds. The staff is often used as a divining rod.

Applying to a shaman

Being able to apply to a shaman for help is simply part of the traditional interpretation of the phenomena of everyday occurrences. For the peoples of the north it is another of the facts of life that have questions hanging over them – such as to what extent the fertility of humans and the reproductive capacities of animals is dependent on the liberality of the spirit-masters (the providers of spirit-souls and of the 'energies' of fertility and reproduction); whether death represents the beginning of a stage the spirit-soul has to undertake in the Lower World; or whether disease is caused by the intervention of a spirit inside the body of a person or – in the case of a serious illness – by the forcible possessing of the spirit-soul itself by some malevolent spirit. It is a fact that certain peoples of Siberia do attribute disease in infants to the vengeance of the spirit of fire following some sin committed earlier by a member of the family. (There are many taboos linked with fire – including pouring water on one, or throwing into the flames any weapon capable of injuring a person.)

In former times, anxiety not to offend the spirits, not to commit any sins against them, was a significant cause of tension in Siberian communities, where nervous disorders were consequently quite common (and where it was for the shaman to deal with them). The result of such tensions in north-eastern Siberia was sometimes – all too often – suicide.

By tradition, then, the aboriginal peoples of Siberia believe misfortune to stem directly from a malevolent disposition of the spirits against them, or as a punishment inflicted by those same spirits on humans after they fail in their religious duties and obligations. To apply to a shaman is therefore to acknowledge that a potentially catastrophic situation has arisen either for a group (famine, epidemic, storm, etc.) or for one of its members (disease, barrenness, unsuccessful hunting, etc.).

210 Tobacco-pouch. Evenki, Yenisey Province, 1913. Coth, glass beads, pearls, hide. Length: 25 cm, width: 13 cm.

Making the application

To make a formal application for help to a shaman, the aboriginal peoples of Siberia have to observe strict rules. They must not, for example, have anything to do with matters that are personal to the shaman (unless, of course, they are themselves part of the shaman's family group). In some areas people send a riding-animal (reindeer or horse) to the shaman and address their requests to him by means of ritualized formulas. Among the Kets, a man who needs the services of the shaman proceeds to the shaman's house, enters and, without saying a word, hangs a piece of white cloth on the wall opposite the doorway. If the shaman can do nothing for him on that day, he takes down the piece of cloth and gives it back to the supplicant without explanation.

Shamanic arenas

Shamanic sessions and séances take place in different types of location – in an enclosed space or an open area, within an ordinary household (in the case of a disease, for example) or in the shamanic residence. In the open, the shaman always chooses a site that symbolizes the conjunction of the three Worlds (with a river, a tree and so forth). But whatever the nature of the location selected for the séance, the space is organized in such a way as to reproduce – as closely as the shaman can make it – the principal characteristics of the structure of the cosmos, as the shaman sees them. The *choom* or the yurt of a shaman is accordingly much larger than those of others. The doorway is usually oriented towards the east. To symbolize the linking of the three Worlds, a pillar (most often made in young birchwood) is erected at the centre of operations. Set thus within the hearth and ascending right through the roof, this axis of the universe has tapered notches that represent the three levels one on top of the other.

Among the Aleuts, the number of notches carved in the pillar instead corresponds to the number of psychic levels the shaman will have to pass through in order to reach the level at which the spirit to whom the ritual is addressed resides.

Primary principles of a séance

Very much at the centre of all shamanic proceedings is a first-object linked to certain 'energies' – 'spirit-souls', 'forces', 'fertility', 'chance' and others. In response to a particular request from applicants, the shaman sets up the shamanic séance, in the course of which he travels – accompanied by all the attributes of his function – either to seek out and track down the 'energies' in the world of spirits that are desired by the applicants, or to expel other 'energies' from the world of humans by removing them to the world of spirits. A shamanic séance is thus intended to re-establish an equilibrium in relations between humans and spirits that has been disrupted. It effects this by transferring, voluntarily or involuntarily, 'energies' currently in the human world to the world of spirits, or conversely, 'energies' currently with the spirits to the human world.

211 Ritual spoon and cup-boat. Eskimo (Uit), Chukchi Peninsula. Walrus ivory. Spoon length: 12.7 cm, cup-boat length: 10.3 cm, height of the cup: 2.2 cm.

212 Koryak woman preparing to cook the meat of a reindeer that has been sacrificed.

A shamanic séance

In order to represent the different stages of his journey, his communication with the spirits and the result of his negotiations with them, the shaman may have recourse to any of a number of procedures. He may beat his drum, chant invocations and use his voice to imitate others (sometimes by ventriloquizing). He may make body-movements so as to dance, to enter a trance, to leap up and down, to pantomime situations, to simulate galloping or flight through the air. And, meanwhile, his assistants are there to understand what is going on, or at least to interpret his actions.

Every shamanic séance begins with an invocation of the shaman's own spirit-protectors. Chanting and beating his drum, the shaman proclaims their names and announces the reason for his invoking them. The spirit-protectors have then to take possession of the shaman's body and all his attributes – a process betokened by much leaping up and down, by convulsions, or by redoubled beating of the drum.

Next, having consulted his spirit-protectors on how the operation should proceed, the shaman embarks on his journey through the different levels of the universe. Each level forms the subject of a chant and a mime, to the beat of the drum. When he finally reaches the spirit or deity that he has been looking for, the shaman introduces himself, reveals the aim of the visitation and enters into negotiations (in which the spectators may be signalled to take part).

Having heard the shaman's entreaty, the spirit may then (as expressed through the mouth of the shaman) demand some sort of remuneration from the humans – offerings, perhaps, or a sacrifice – or may simply refuse the request.

Then the shaman returns to the Earth, with or without the desired 'energy'. He tells the applicants how the negotiations turned out, gives a prediction of how the situation (which prompted the séance) will develop and/or be resolved, and any accompanying conditions. And if he can, he transmits to the applicants the 'energy' he has received. The séance ends with the departure of his spirit-protectors.

This overall structure and the general principles which support it represent the basis of every shamanic séance. There are additional factors, on the other hand, which may vary in significance. They include the nature of the spirit to whom the entreaty is addressed (a spirit-master who may be favourable to the request of the human applicants); the nature of the 'energy' desired by the applicants and sought after by the shaman; the nature of the remuneration demanded by the spirits (in exchange for services rendered).

213 Woman cleaning the bones of a reindeer sacrificed during the traditional festival of the Koryak reindeer-herders.

214 Carved miniature: 'Cutting off the head of a reindeer'. Koryak, Kamchatka, 1911. Walrus ivory, length: 6 cm, width: 6.5 cm.

215 Yakut calendars. 1906. Wood, i) diameter: 6 cm, ii) length: 15.2 cm, width: 11.5 cm.

216 Preparing a cow's head. Central
Yakutia.

217 The Eveni rite of the spirits of water, performed during the summer festival of The Minor Peoples of the North. Yakutsk.

218 Ceremony at sunrise at the beginning of the traditional Yakut festival of Isahar.

219 The dance *ohuokhai*, the Yakut festival of Isahar.

Shamanic séances to treat illness

In the case of illness, the close relatives of the affected person together make an appeal to the shaman begging him to intercede with the spirit responsible for the disorder.

Most commonly, the operation consists of getting rid of a malevolent spirit that has intruded into the body of the sick person. Procedures for removing the source of the problem are numerous. Having narrowed down exactly where in the body of the sick person the spirit responsible for the disorder is located, the shaman may draw it out by sucking with his mouth or through a tube (for example, a hollow bone); he may drive it out by beating on his drum; or he may lure it out with the appetizing aroma of food. Once extracted from the body, the spirit is at once confined in some sort of container-object put by specially for the purpose (a box, a doll, a pot, or something) to be thrown away or to be kept until the cure is seen to be complete, according to the shaman's directions.

In the case of serious illness, the shaman has actually to go out and search for the spirit-soul of the affected person (which has been possessed by a spirit). He must look for it in the different levels of the World, find it, bring it back, and re-install it within the sick individual. At that final stage there are various procedures surrounding the reintroduction of the spirit-soul into the body. The shaman can make it return via the head with a beat of his drum; he can blow it in at the ear or at the mouth; or he can have it confined in special container-objects (figurines, small items, stones, insects, whatever) to be kept carefully by the sick individual.

The role of the shaman at a funeral

Among the peoples of the north, the death of a person occasions quite a number of different rites and rituals designed to expedite the transition of the spirit-soul of the deceased down to the Lower World. In certain circumstances these rites and rituals are performed by the shaman; in others they are performed by the deceased's family and relatives. Initially, the spirit-soul of the deceased is commonly kept within some sort of container-object for a set period of time (which varies from some minutes to several years). Among the Evenki, for example, the shaman retrieves the spirit-soul of the deceased and lodges it within a carved figurine filled with rotten wood, gives it food and tobacco, then accompanies it back to the kingdom of the dead. Among the Nanai people it is on the seventh day after death that the shamans breathe the spirit-soul of the deceased into a cushion-cover, where it stays for a period of three years. At the end of this time a shaman accompanies the deceased's spirit-soul once and for all to the Underworld.

220 Wrestling-match for Chukchis during a festival.

221 Man's festive trousers, seen from the front. Koryak, Kamchatka, 1909–1911. Sealskin and -fur, alder bark, reindeer-hair. Length: 101 cm, width at the belt: 48 cm.

222 Man's festive trousers, seen from the back. Koryak, Kamchatka, 1909–1911. Sealskin and -fur, alder bark, cloth, reindeer-hair. Length: 101 cm, width at the belt: 48 cm.

223 'Aerial' coffin. Yakut, beginning of
the 20th century.

224 Tomb of an ancestor. Evenki,
beginning of the 20th century.

Requests for children

Faced with a request of this nature, a shaman of the Evenki people arranges a séance in the course of which he returns to the human world spirit-souls that have been situated on a plane a little lower than the Upper World. Spirit-souls from there have the appearance of little birds flittering from branch to branch. Without its noticing, the shaman picks out one of them, and brings it very quickly back with him to Earth. There, the shaman sets the spirit-soul bird down at the centre of a white cloth held at the four corners by four children (two boys and two girls) who quickly enfold it in the cloth so that the spirit-soul cannot escape. The spirit-soul wrapped up in this way is put inside a box for safe keeping and the shaman goes on to tell the would-be parents that they should soon be expecting a child . . .

Among the Altai people, couples who have experienced repeated stillbirths come to talk to the shaman and to beg him to intercede with the spirits in their favour so that future babies may be hardier and survive. To try to ensure that, the shaman has to deliver to the spirits the placentas from the stillbirths (placentas are traditionally buried under the household hearth after births) and obtain in exchange from them other placentas from families whose babies grew in perfect health. The 'new' placentas then take the place of the old ones under the hearth of the couple making the request.

Requests for material prosperity

Men often ask the shaman to improve their luck when going hunting or fishing, or for an increase of numbers in their herd. The principle behind the shaman's work in such cases is to trace the spirit-master concerned with such a request and to get from him permission to use the 'forces' or the 'spirit-souls' required to bring them back to Earth and to insert them into the natural environment at appropriate sites (thus also effectively symbolizing the much-desired renewal of natural resources). He might, for example, scatter hairs from the hides of game hunted by men in the taiga, or cast fish-scales in the waters of rivers and lakes.

225 Stick to beat out the sins from the bodies of the dead. Koryak, Kamchatka, 1956. Ram's-horn, ****, length: 43.5 cm, width: 5.5 cm.

226 Tombs in the taiga. Yakutia.

RITES AND RITUALS

The traditional lifestyle of the peoples of Siberia is punctuated with rites and rituals, feasts and festivals which are firmly linked to economic, social and family cycles and which (among other things) govern the behaviour of individuals within communities, influence relations between groups and affect the scheduling of food-production activities. Badly disrupted by Soviet domination, the traditional system has nonetheless been important in ensuring the transmitting of ancestral cultures from generation to generation.

Undertaken individually or collectively, by the people together or by shamans on their behalf, the rituals have just the same objectives as do shamanic séances – the re-establishing of natural order, the restoration of the equilibrium of natural forces, the elimination of the sources of harm and misfortune, the guaranteeing of future wellbeing…

Rites and rituals involving magic

Rites and rituals that involve magic still have a secure place in the everyday lives of the peoples of Siberia. While hunting, the Chuckchis constantly murmur magical spells in the firm belief that only the target animals or spirits can hear them. When they go walrus hunting, therefore, this is the kind of thing they may repeat over and over again: 'O

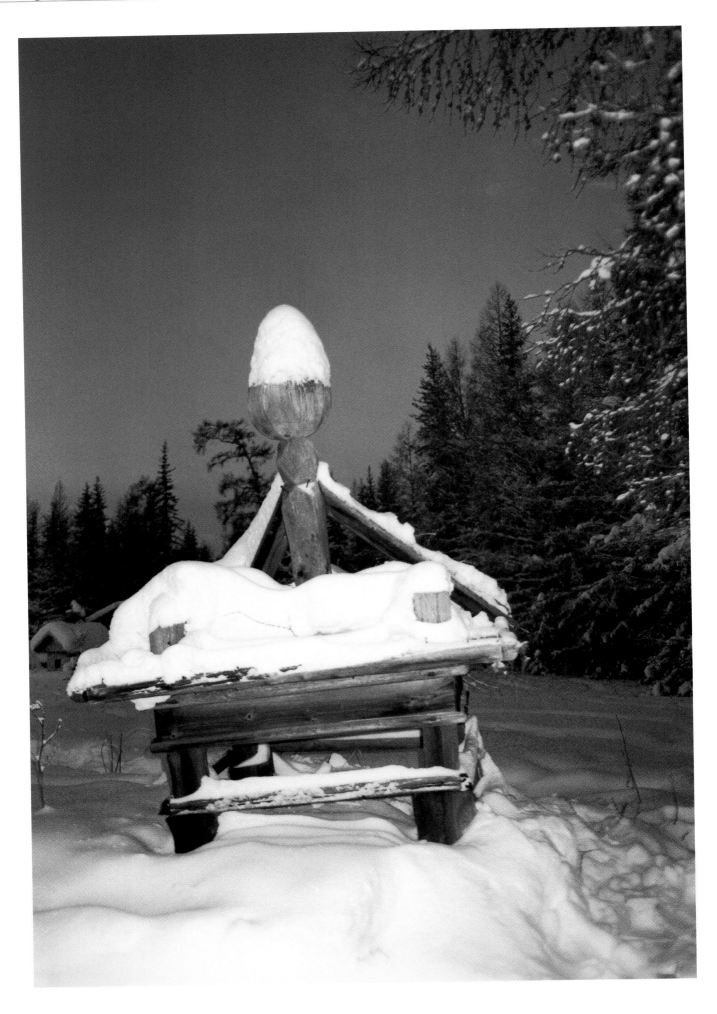

walruses, I hold a great sheet of iron over your ears so that you may not hear the swishing paddle-strokes of my bidarka.'

Many prohibitions and taboos affect the behaviour of hunters on land. If a hunter is going to speak at all, he must, for example, speak plainly but modestly – and yet it is utterly forbidden for him to pronounce the word that describes the animal he is hunting. Such restrictions have as much to do with the possibility of frightening away the game as with belief in the magical ability of the animals (and their spirit-masters) to hear and to understand the words of men.

While the men are out hunting, the behaviour of their nearest and dearest is also subject to a good many restrictions and taboos. Chukchi wives left in their shoreline homes are obliged to utter spells designed to urge sea creatures towards the hunters. Among the Nivkhi, when their men are hunting in the forests, the wives must under no circumstances embroider anything using the traditional arabesque pattern (which may cause the hunters to lose the spoor and strike off in all directions, like the pattern). Nor may they knead dough (which may cause the hunters to go blind) or sing (or the game-animals will run away), for example. When the hunters return empty-handed, then, it is certainly not unknown for them to imply that the fault lies with those who stayed at home in the village!

Rituals related to food production

In order to optimise the quantity of game taken in the hunt, the number of fish caught, or the size of the herds of livestock reared, the aboriginal peoples of Siberia perform different rituals according to a calendar that focuses mainly on economic necessities.

The Evenki perform their hunting ritual in this way: before leaving for the forest, each hunter 'feeds' his hearth by throwing a lump of animal fat upon the fire. He then takes up the *belleyi*, a figurine that represents the coming hunt – a humanoid shape that has legs and a head with eyes, mouth and nose, but has no arms – and passes it through the smoke before brandishing it over the hearth's earth surface. He begs the earth to help him in the hunt, promising it a reward if it does so. To complete the ritual, the hunter lets the figurine drop to the ground. Depending on which way up it comes to rest, he can estimate what his chances are of returning with success or failure.

227 Tomb in the taiga. Yakutia.

228 Sculpture: wrestling, playing chess and shooting for the post. Koryak, beginning of the 20th century.

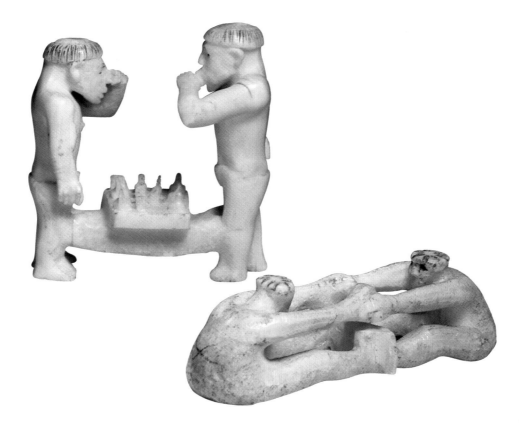

229 Mortuary costume of a man, seen from the back. Koryak, Kamchatka, 1904–1911. Reindeer-hide, dog-skin, sealskin, alder bark, reindeer-hair. Length of the *kukhlianka*: 98 cm, width at its bottom: 94 cm.

230 Mortuary costume of a man, seen from the front. Koryak, Kamchatka, 1904–1911. Reindeer-hide, dog-skin, sealskin, alder bark, reindeer-skin. Length of the *kukhlianka*: 98 cm, length of trousers: 86 cm, length of footwear: 23 cm, width of *kukhlianka* at the bottom: 94 cm, height of the boots: 17 cm.

Among the coastal groups, preparations for walrus hunting begin with a ritual known as the launching of the bidarkas. It takes place at the beginning of spring, at the time of the main thaw. On the day of the ritual, early in the morning, the villagers run at full tilt down to the seashore. A fire is lit and 'fed' to become a sacred flame. Then the fishermen take down their bidarkas – laid out for the winter, strapped down with leather thongs on supports at some height off the ground – and carry them with great care towards the edge of the water. There, they cover them with a thick layer of snow. Offerings are solemnly brought to them on plates, of reindeer-meat and lumps of fat, which are deposited at the ends of the bidarkas. Throughout, the ceremony is accompanied by very slow and very rhythmic dancing intended as an appeal to the nearby sea always to be as calm and as rhythmically peaceful. Then the best hunters take themselves off to one side of the assembly and, amid general silence, address the spirits of the sea, calling upon them to bear witness to their respect . . . and asking for abundant catches. The entire ritual is performed with the utmost scrupulousness and attention to detail, for it is the hunters' belief that their success over the whole hunting season depends totally upon this ceremony.

Rituals surrounding the deaths of animals

Every animal killed – as the result of hunting or of slaughter from the herd – is the object of ritual ceremonies designed to preserve its spirit-soul and to restore it to its spirit-master. So, for example, when a fur-bearing animal is captured and killed, its nose, lips and eyes (in which the spirit-soul is believed to reside) are removed first and either left there on the ground surface or buried on the spot. In this way, the animal's spirit-soul may be returned to its original environment.

Ceremonies of this kind take place as and when appropriate to specific events – to celebrate a kill by an individual or a group – or by regulation of a calendar, as an annual event or festival.

Rituals designed to ensure the restoration of the spirit-soul of animals to their spirit-masters consist mainly – though not entirely – of the performance of 'magical' dances together with eulogies addressed to the animals and about those same animals, regarding them not as the victims of men but as the esteemed hosts of the ceremony, appealing to them to be reborn, to come back once more as quickly as they may.

The peoples of the Pacific coasts – the Chukchis, Aleuts and Uit (Eskimos) - venerate the whale. After a successful whale hunt, all the inhabitants of a village rush down to the shore to welcome the animal. While the huge body is being cut into pieces, fiery torches are lit and magical spells are declaimed. Then the head of the whale is cut off. From that point on, the head – although separated from the rest of the body – represents the whole animal. The hunters 'feed' it, then later, during the night-time, take it to one of the houses in the village. Addressing it with great respect, the villagers implore it to tell other whales of the extremely warm welcome it has received and to suggest they should come forward to meet humans for themselves. Its fat is smeared on amulets and used to 'feed' the fire in the hearth. After the ceremony its shoulder blades are used to predict the future. And five days later it is finally time to say goodbye to the whale. In a rite that requires the women present to cover their faces with a mask of grasses, the spirit-soul of the whale is sent back home. Afterwards, the men believe that this ritual has ensured that whale hunts in the future will always turn out to be successful.

Sacrifices

Sacrifices and offerings – generally motivated by aspirations or fears in relation to the abundance of game and/or fish, to the numbers of livestock reared or to good fortune in hunting – are based on the principle of 'exchange' between the world of humans and the world of the spirit-masters. Effectively, in a sacrifice, the humans feel themselves obliged to offer the spirit-masters something they think the spirit-masters don't have, something they think the spirit-masters must want. For example, in making a sacrifice to the spirit-master of the taiga, it is not possible to offer up anything else than an animal that counts as domestic livestock (a reindeer, a horse, other horned animals, a dog…) or one or more fish.

In any case, it is possible to honour the spirits other than with blood-sacrifices, by making offerings of household items, e.g., clothing, food.

Where a blood-sacrifice is obligatory, however, humans must take great care not to imperil the spirit-soul of the animal but to ensure that it reaches the petitioned spirits in pristine condition. Most often, the animal is despatched by cutting through the aorta (the large blood vessel leading from the heart) and the blood is collected. The blood and other parts of the animal's corpse thought to contain the spirit-soul (the skin, the claws, the head, the hoofs) are then offered to the spirits, while its flesh is shared out between the members of the sacrificial party.

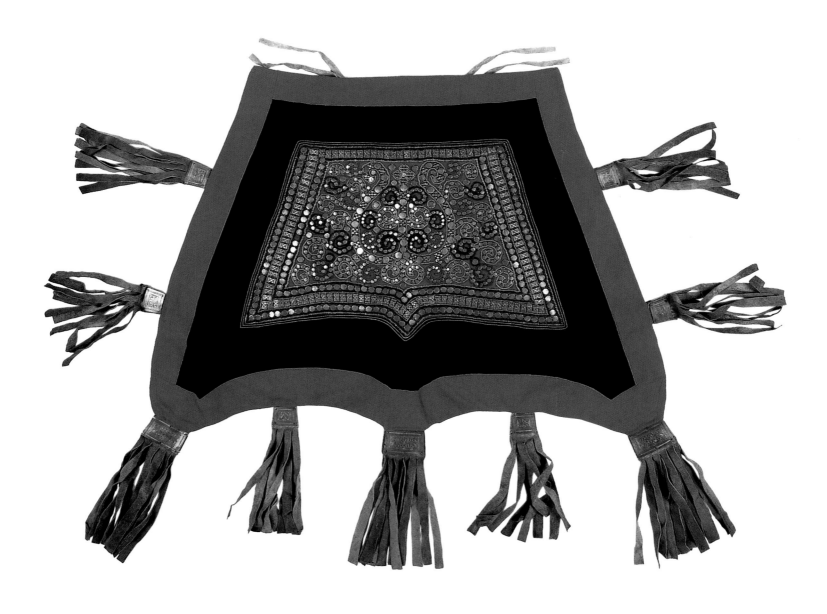

231 Shabrack: the covering for a
horse's crupper. Yakut, Yakutsk, 1959.
Cloth, metal, glass beads, cured hide
(leather). Length: 74 cm, width:
101 cm.

Calendrical feasts and festivals

For many of the peoples of Siberia, the traditional start of the year is around the summer solstice – midsummer day, 20–24 June. The festivals that take place then not unnaturally resemble our New Year festivals, representing a celebration of the opening of a new cycle of life, a reflowering of nature after the long and bitter winter.

Isyakh

It is the Yakuts who celebrate the festival known as Isyakh, which takes place at around 20 June and begins at dawn with a welcome for the sun. The ceremony is organized and directed by a 'white' shaman (although there are also 'black' shamans). Facing towards the rising sun, the shaman divides the people massed behind him into sections with men on his right and women on his left. At the first rays of sunshine he lights a fire, 'feeds' it, then sprinkles the ground nearby with *koumiss* (fermented mare's milk) while continually intoning ritual incantations to the deities of the sky. On behalf of the assembled people he asks the gods for prosperity (in both economic and material senses) and fertility. Once the sun is above the horizon, the women on their side, and the men on theirs, form circles and begin to dance the *osukhay*, all the while calling out words and phrases in homage to the gods. The real festivities begin immediately afterwards and last for three days. The only breaks are for dances and sporting competitions, and it all ends with horseraces.

Peg-hitin

After the winter solstice – midwinter, 24 December to 6 January – the Koryak and Chukchi reindeer-herders organize a festival in celebration of the constellation Peg-hitin, which is held in special veneration among the nomads of north-eastern Siberia. It is at this time of the year that the stars Altair and Tarazed in what we know as the constellation Aquila appear in the heavens as part of the larger constellation they call Peg-hitin, so signalling the beginning of new life after the long Arctic night. Various events characterize the festivities: reindeer are sacrificed in honour of Peg-hitin, races are held between teams of reindeer and there are wrestling and ice-pillar-climbing contests. In an ice-pillar-climbing contest it is traditional for the first to make it all the way to the top of the pillar to salute the sun with joyful exclamations.

The festival of 'the purified choom'

At the end of the long Arctic night, when the sun begins to peer above the horizon once more, the Nganassani people celebrate the festival they know as that of 'the purified choom'. Under the direction of a shaman, this celebration lasts from three to nine days, and joins together a number of clans whose members all wear special festival clothing. Unlike ordinary clothing, these costumes have nothing on them to show the wearer's social or civic status. Moreover, the costumes enable people to come into contact with the spirits and/or to pass into a new stage in their lives.

232 Carving of a bear.

Rites of passage

Today largely forgotten, rites of passage used very clearly to mark essential stages in the lives of most people in ethnic communities in Siberia. The most important of them were those that concerned birth and death.

Births

When pregnant, women were subject to various prohibitions and taboos. Among certain peoples (including the Nanai people and the Evenki), a pregnant woman was obliged to leave the family residence and live in solitude until her baby was born. This period of isolation was considered necessary because of the traditional interpretation of pregnancy: just as the hunter left to go hunting in the forest, or the shaman left to seek help on other planes, a woman once pregnant should 'leave to go searching' for the spirit-soul of her baby, and to fetch it from the spirit-masters.

Bearing this interpretation in mind makes it possible to understand how a whole collection of rites and rituals came to surround the process of childbirth. For example, the area in which the birth was to happen had to be organized and arranged into a place where the world of humans and the world of the natural sphere might properly meet.

Before the confinement, the mother-to-be would 'entertain' the spirit-protectors of her clan. The birth would take place in the presence of a wise woman aided by her spirit-protectors and armed with good luck charms, including perhaps the umbilical cord of her own mother. The intention was to guarantee favourable contact between the mother-to-be and the spirit or deity of birth (known as Yamyunia to the Nenets, Ayeeus-sut to the Yakuts, and A-nay to the Altai people).

Following the birth of the child, many rituals celebrated the baby's passage from the natural sphere to the social sphere. One such ritual comprised the symbolic restoration of the placenta (considered to be another form of the same child) back to nature – a ritual that ensured the possibility of further pregnancies in due course.

Funerals

Before the Russians arrived, the peoples of north-eastern Siberia did not bury their dead. The permafrost saw to it that burying anything, even a corpse, was not a practical proposition anywhere in Siberia except in the south. In the tundra, the dead might be taken to a remote spot and left to their own devices, either in the open or under a cairn of stones. Elsewhere, they might be placed inside 'aerial' coffins propped up on some sort of supporting framework or suspended from the branches of trees. And in certain areas of the south, the extreme east and the north-east of Siberia, cremation was the rule.

Funerary rituals tend to conform to an inversion of the rituals surrounding childbirth. Relatives make certain ritual hand gestures over the body, spend some time in contemplative remembrance with it and then take it from the house (usually through an opening made specially) to its place of burial. There, sacrifices and offerings are made. Then the deceased is prepared for his or her future existence. The corpse is surrounded by all the things he or she might need in the Lower World – clothes, items of property, animals… Occasionally, the deceased and these things undergo a final transformation together (by way of incineration or other forms of physical destruction). At the end of these funerary observances, the deceased is considered to have become a new person and is even referred to under a new name. To pronounce the former names of those now dead is taboo.

There follows a period of commemoration for the dead person. Its duration depends on local tradition, but may be of several weeks to several years. (It lasts 49 days among the Tuva people, seven years among the Enets.) For this length of time, the aboriginal peoples of Siberia think of the spirit-soul of the deceased as roaming through the favourite places of his or her old life and putting matters to rights once and for all. On each occasion the relatives visit the burial site for a further commemorative ritual; they offer the dead person food, clothing and other items meant to assist in preparing him or her for the time of departure to the Lower World. The time at last comes for the period of commemoration to end. Denoting the final passage of the spirit-soul of the deceased to its new realm, the Underworld, a ceremony may be performed under the aegis of a shaman via a séance or be held privately by the deceased's nearest relatives.

*

THE SONG OF THE SHAMAN

(BY V.A DOLGOUNOV)

Hoyaw-koo! Hoyaw-koo!
My spirit, my Master,
My companion, my likeness,
Spirit-soul,
Take possession of your mistress,
Of your beautiful grandmother –
Stir with all your strength,
Shaking her until she starts frothing,
Beating her until she bubbles over.

Hoyaw-koo! Hoyaw-koo!
A dread misfortune will surge forward.
A feared misfortune is about to break.
A great misfortune has come to shore.

Hoyaw-koo! Hoyaw-koo!
You who act as shaman in this great tidal roar,
My beloved little father,
My protective shell,
My loyal helper –
If you can manage it of yourself,
What do you say?
What is the price I will have to pay?

Hoyaw-koo! Hoyaw-koo!
My little mouse of a shaman,
My dearest sister,
My protective shell,
My loyal helper –
If you can manage it of yourself,

What do you say?
What is the price that I will have to pay?
Hoyaw-koo! Hoyaw-koo!
You who lived so gloriously in times now gone,
My poor little grandmother,
To confront what afflicts us now,
If you can manage it of yourself,
What do you say?
What is the price I will have to pay?

Hoyaw-koo! Hoyaw-koo!
My mistress,
You, my beautiful grandmother –
Skimming the surface of the water,
Riding on one of the white horses,
Flying above the liquid ice,
Sporting a badge at his harness-breast,
With a watch on his wrist,
With a mirror in his pocket,
Holding the law in his clenched hand,
Reading his destiny from his palm,
A blade hooked into his sword-belt,
It is your Prince of Amyhaakh.

If from his wife,
Spirit-soul,
From the white and opaline Me-khe-jay
I manage to get through to myself,
Even if I die,
I will not be looking for death.

Hoyaw-koo! Hoyaw-koo!
My very own little bird –
Darting its eyes all around,
Shining with all its fiery light,
It can be seen on the plain
With its steaming breath,
With its loud neighing,
With its gleaming caparison:
Even if I owned such a horse,
What would happen then?

Hoyaw-koo! Hoyaw-koo!
It can be seen in the byre,
With its shaggy coat,
With its well-curved back,
With its horns thrusting forward,
With its flattened hooves:
Even if I owned such a cow,
What would happen then?

Hoyaw-koo! Hoyaw-koo!
It can be seen in the taiga,
Treading with a step that snaps,
With its soft fur,
Feeding on mosses,

With hooves from which combs are made,
With antlers on the top of its head:
Even if I owned such a reindeer,
What would happen then?

Hoyaw-koo! Hoyaw-koo!
Even if I had clothing that was
Threadbare through being worn,
Even if I had money
That goes and that comes,
Even if I had coins
Stamped with the Eagle,
What would happen then?

Hoyaw-koo! Hoyaw-koo!
See how I am now,
With my face all pale,
With my brittle bones,
With a feeble tread –
Isn't that how I am?
With fat cheeks,
With a bulbous Russian nose –
See the man that I am!

Hoyaw-koo! Hoyaw-koo!

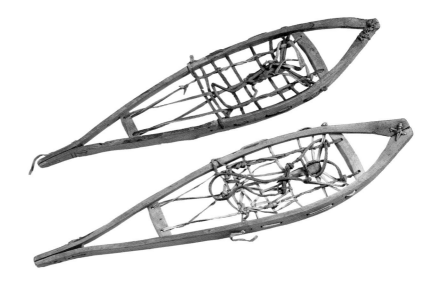

233 Chukchi snow-shoes. The Anadyr area, 1904–1907. Wood, sealskin, length: 75.7 cm, width: 19 cm.

THE PEOPLES OF SIBERIA

ALEUTS

Number: nearly 2,000 in the USA; 700 in Russia
Location: Aleutian Islands (south-west of Alaska, USA, towards Kamchatka); Commander (Komandorski) Islands (Russia: Bering Sea)
Livelihood: residential; hunting sea mammals, fishing
Religion: shamanism
Language: (Eskimo-)Aleut group

BURYATS

Number: 421,000 in Russia; 70,000 in Mongolia; small communities in the north-east of China
Location: around Lake Baikal; Republic of Buryatia; Autonomous Buryat District of Ust' Orda in Irkutsk Oblast; Autonomous Buryat District of Aga in Chita Oblast
Livelihood: Mongolian-style nomadic rearing (of cattle, horses, sheep, goats, camels) to the east of Lake Baikal; semi-residential rearing to the west
Religion: Buddhism in the east; shamanism in the west
Language: Mongolian family

CHUKCHIS (THE CHUKCHI PEOPLE)

Number: 15,000
Location: Autonomous District of the Chukchis; the northern part of the Autonomous District of the Koryaks; the north-east of Yakutia
Livelihood: Ankalynes of the coastal area, residential: hunting of marine mammals; Chaochus of the tundra, nomadic: reindeer-herding
Religion: shamanism
Language: Chukchi-Koryak-Kamchadal group

DOLGANS (THE DOLGAN PEOPLE)

Number: 6,945
Location: northern Yakutia, the Taimyr Peninsula
Livelihood: semi-residential; reindeer-herding, hunting, fishing
Religion: Orthodox Christianity; elements of shamanism
Language: Turkic family

EVENI (THE EVENI PEOPLE; THE LAMUT)

Number: 17,000
Location: north-eastern Yakutia; Khabarovsk Region; Chukotka; Kamchatka
Livelihood: nomadic in the tundra; reindeer-herding and -hunting semi-residential in coastal areas; fishing, hunting marine mammals
Religion: shamanism
Language: Tungusic family

EVENKI (THE EVENKI PEOPLE)

Number: 30,164
Location: Autonomous District of the Evenki (Krasnoyarsk Oblast); Khabarovsk Region; the Republics of Yakutia and Buryatia, in Irkutsk, Chita and Amur Oblasts
Livelihood: nomadic; reindeer-herding and -hunting
Religion: shamanism
Language: Tungusic family

KETS (THE KET PEOPLE; 'YENISEY-OSTYAKS')

Number: 1,113
Location: strip centring on the Yenisey River south of Turukhansk, Baikit Oblast (Krasnoyarsk Region)
Livelihood: residential; hunting and fishing
Religion: shamanism
Language: apparently unrelated

KHANTY (THE KHANTY PEOPLE; OSTYAKS)

Number: 22,521
Location: Autonomous District of the Khanty-Mansi; Autonomous District of the Yamal-Nenets, Tomsk Oblast
Livelihood: nomadic reindeer-herding in the tundra – hunting and fishing in the taiga; rearing of various animals (goats, sheep, pigs, etc.) in southerly areas and on the Ob River
Religion: shamanism; bear cults
Language: Finno-Ugric family

KORYAKS

Number: 9,000
Location: Autonomous District of the Koryaks; Autonomous District of the Chukchis, Magadan Oblast
Livelihood: nomadic reindeer-herding in the tundra; residential fishing and hunting of marine mammals in coastal areas
Religion: shamanism
Language: Chukchi-Koryak-Kamchadal group

MANSIS (THE MANSI PEOPLE; THE VOGUL PEOPLE)

Number: 8,474
Location: Autonomous District of the Khanty-Mansi
Livelihood: hunting and fishing; reindeer-herding now almost died out
Religion: shamanism
Language: Finno-Ugric family

THE NANAI PEOPLE (THE GOLD PEOPLE)

Number: 12,000 in Russia; around 1,000 in China
Location: the extreme east of Russia, in the lower course of the Amur River (the Regions of Khabarovsk and of the Primor'ye); the island of Sakhalin
Livelihood: residential; hunting and fishing
Religion: shamanism
Language: Tungusic family

THE NEGIDAL PEOPLE

Number: 622
Location: the lower course of the Amur River (Khabarovsk Region)
Livelihood: residential; hunting and fishing
Religion: shamanism; bear cults
Language: Tungusic family

THE NENETS

Number: 34,000
Location: Autonomous Districts of the Nenets (Archangel Oblast), of the Yamal-Nenets, and of the Dolgan-Nenets
Livelihood: nomadic; reindeer-herding in the taiga and the tundra
Religion: shamanism
Language: Samoyedic family

NIVKHI (THE NIVKHI PEOPLE; GILYAKS)

Number: 4,673
Location: the lower course of the Amur River; the island of Sakhalin
Livelihood: residential; fishing, hunting, hunting of marine mammals; crop-farming, rearing of dogs
Religion: shamanism; bear cults
Language: apparently unrelated

OLCHI (THE OLCHI PEOPLE)

Number: 3,200
Location: the extreme east of Russia, in the lower course of the Amur River (Khabarovsk Region)
Livelihood: residential; hunting and fishing
Religion: shamanism; bear cults
Language: Tungusic family

THE OROCHON PEOPLE

Number: 915
Location: Khabarovsk Region, Amur Oblast
Livelihood: residential; hunting and fishing
Religion: shamanism
Language: Tungusic family

OROKI (THE OROKI PEOPLE)

Number: 190
Location: the island of Sakhalin
Livelihood: semi-residential; fishing and the hunting of marine mammals in coastal areas; hunting in the taiga
Religion: shamanism
Language: Tungusic family

THE TUVA PEOPLE (TUVINIANS; THE URYANKHAI; THE SOYOT)

Number: 235,000
Location: Republic of Tuva (south of Siberia on the border with Mongolia, between the Ob and Yenisey Rivers); Mongolia; China
Livelihood: nomadic; horse-, cattle- and camel-breeding
Religion: Tibetan Buddhism (Lamaism); shamanism
Language: Turkic family

UDEKHE (THE UDEKHE PEOPLE)

Number: 2,011
Location: the Regions of Khabarovsk and of the Primor'ye
Livelihood: residential; hunting and fishing
Religion: shamanism; tiger cults
Language: Tungusic family

UIT (THE YUIT)

Number: (Inuit:) 35,000 in the USA; 26,000 in Canada; 45,000 in Greenland;
(Yuit:) 1,700 in Russia
Location: as above – but in Russia: the eastern side of Chukotka; Wrangell Island
Livelihood: residential; hunting marine mammals, shooting and trapping birds, fishing, crop-farming
Religion: shamanism
Language: Eskimo(-Aleut) group

YAKUTS

Number: 382,000
Location: Republic of Sakha (Yakutia)
Livelihood: residential; rearing of horses and domestic livestock
Religion: shamanism
Language: Turkic family

YUKAGHIRS

Number: 1,142
Location: northern Yakutia, Kolyma and Magadan Oblasts
Livelihood: nomadic and residential; hunting, reindeer-herding, breeding hunting-dogs
Religion: shamanism
Language: Yukaghir-Chuvantsi group

Picture List